剑桥双语分级阅读·小说馆（第2版）

原版系列编辑 Philip Prowse

Berlin Express

柏林快车

[英] 迈克尔·奥斯汀 著

李艳 编译

北京语言大学出版社
BEIJING LANGUAGE AND CULTURE UNIVERSITY PRESS

CAMBRIDGE UNIVERSITY PRESS

社图号25008

图书在版编目（CIP）数据

柏林快车 ： 英汉对照 / （英）迈克尔·奥斯汀（Michael Austen）著 ； 李艳编译. -- 2版. -- 北京 ：北京语言大学出版社，2025. 3. --（剑桥双语分级阅读小说馆）. -- ISBN 978-7-5619-6727-0

Ⅰ. H319.4

中国国家版本馆CIP数据核字第20253ZJ930号

柏林快车
BOLIN KUAICHE

责任编辑：于华颖
责任印制：周 燚

出版发行：北京语言大学出版社
社 址：北京市海淀区学院路 15 号，100083
网 址：www.blcup.com
电子信箱：service@blcup.com
电 话：编 辑 部 010-8230 1019
发 行 部 010-8230 3650/3591/3648
北语书店 010-8230 3653
网购咨询 010-8230 3908
印 刷：东港股份有限公司

版 次：2017 年 6 月第 1 版 2025 年 3 月第 2 版
印 次：2025 年 3 月第 1 次印刷
开 本：880 毫米 × 1230 毫米 1/32
印 张：6.75
字 数：160 千字
定 价：23.00 元

PRINTED IN CHINA
凡有印装质量问题，本社负责调换。售后QQ号1367565611，电话010-82303590

Preface

前言

“剑桥双语分级阅读·小说馆”是一套从剑桥大学出版社引进的面向非英语国家英语学习者的分级系列读物，由英语语言教学专家及小说作家合力创作。创作过程历时三十余年，出版后受到世界各地英语教师和英语学习者的喜爱，许多读本再版多次，三十余年来畅销不衰，成为受全球英语学习者青睐的优秀读本。

本系列读物具有以下突出特色：

1. 是原创英语读物，而非改编自普通作品的读物。因此，阅读本系列读物，我们读到的是原汁原味的原创英语，而非人为改编过的二手英语。

2. 是当代优秀短篇小说，而非年代久远的小说。因此，阅读本系列读物，我们读到的是当今鲜活的、学了就能用的英语，而非穿越时空的、学了用不上的英语；了解的是与读者同时代不同国家人们的生活和思想，而非隔代人的生活、文化和风土人情。

3. 是专为非英语国家的英语学习者量身定制的读物，而非为英语母语者所写的大众读物。因此，本系列读物是中国读者首选的英语学习读物。

4. 是英美知名小说家和英语语言教学专家合力创作的读物。小说家保障了读物的可读性与可欣赏性，英语语言教学专家保障了读物语言作为英语习得材料的科学性与可学性。本系列读物中的多个读本都曾在世界上颇具影响力的“语言学习者文学奖”（Language Learner Literature Award）评选中获得大奖。因此，阅读本系列读物，我们会在欣赏小说的同时，自然而然地、有效地提高自己的英语水平。

5. 本系列读物的故事题材丰富多样，包括侦探、情感、历险、悬疑、人文、科幻、喜剧等，读者可以随心选择自己喜欢的类别阅读；故事内容生动有趣，故事情节引人入胜、扣人心弦，读者一旦开始阅读，就想一口气读完，使阅读真正升华到“悦读”。

6. 随书附赠的音频材料内容精彩，是专业配音员的演绎再创作。听着它，我们犹如在听广播剧、听评书，又仿佛是在听电影、听话剧……这种聆听英语的享受将彻底扫除学生对英语听力的畏难心理。

7. 本系列读物所使用的语言，既有英式英语，也有美式英语，对应的音频材料也相应分为英音和美音，读者可根据自己的喜好来选择。

8. 本系列近百本读物根据《欧洲语言共同参考框架》(CEFR) 和剑桥大学外语考评部开发的 ESOL 考试的标准来确定级别划分，是建立在科学研究和实践基础之上的分级。全套共分七个级别（与中国学生英语基础水平的大致对应关系，请参见图书封底表格），读者可根据自己的英语基础选择相应级别的读本来学习。

为了更好地帮助中国学生学习和欣赏，“剑桥双语分级阅读・小说馆”从剑桥大学出版社原版引进后又增加了以下内容：

1. 增加了适量的辅助学习内容，包括“读前思考”“读后活动”“学习指导”三个板块，其中“学习指导”板块又包括生词、短语和表达、文化点滴、阅读练习四项内容。增加这些板块的目的是全方位帮助学生提升英语阅读能力，扩充词汇量，扫除阅读中的文化障碍，增强对英语小说的鉴赏能力。

2. 增加了小说全文的参考译文。出于语言学习的考虑，译文多采用直译，但也尽量符合中文的表达习惯。

值得一提的是，所增加的辅助学习内容和参考译文，全部由来自全国不同省市知名中学（包括人大附中、北大附中、清华附中、黄冈中学、上海中学等三十余所中学）的一线英语教师完成。这些一线教师的加盟，确保了所加内容与中国学生的英语学习特点和学习需求相吻合，为学生阅读和欣赏读物、提高英语水平给予恰到好处的助力。

英语阅读是英语课堂的延伸和补充，也是培养英语语感、提高英语水平的有效途径。选择一套好的英语读物，收获的将不仅仅是语言的进步。欢迎年轻朋友们来到“剑桥双语分级阅读·小说馆”，打开一本本好书，品味一个个好故事，为实现梦想搭建桥梁。

北京语言大学出版社

Contents 目录

People in the story

故事中的人物

Hiro Adachi: a Japanese university student, studying in England

足立宏：一个在英国学习的日本大学生

Akiko: Hiro's ex-girlfriend

秋子：宏的前女友

The Shark / Erik Björnson: an old man Hiro meets on the train

鲨鱼 / 埃里克·比约恩森：宏在火车上遇到的一个老头儿

Karl Meier: a German man in Berlin

卡尔·迈耶：一个来自柏林的德国人

Franz Schubert: a bodyguard

弗朗兹·舒伯特：一名保镖

Before reading

读前思考

1. Look at the front cover of the book. What does the picture show, and how does it relate to the title?
2. Read the blurb on the back cover. Who is the main character? Why is he in Berlin?
3. According to the blurb, how does the story start?
4. If this happened to you, what would you do?
5. Look at the list of characters on pages 2 and 3. How do you think they are connected?
6. If you have the recording, listen to Chapter 1.

Chapter 1
The past and the future

The train was really flying along now. The buildings, fields and trees all seemed to race by. A bridge shot past the window. Then a station. Hiro put his face nearer the glass to see the name, but they were travelling so fast it was impossible to read. Hiro wondered if they were travelling faster than the *Shinkansen*, the world-famous Bullet Train of Japan. He looked up at the small screen above the door, which showed the speed – 294 kilometres per hour! He watched the numbers as they slowly increased. 296 ... 298 ... All of a sudden, they were there: 301 kph! Well, that was something exciting to tell ...

And then it hit him all over again. Yes, but who would he tell? If it had been a month ago - even two weeks - he would have sent Akiko a text. But since their break-up she didn't want to hear from him. 'Don't send me any messages, because I won't reply,' she had told him angrily. 'If you'd rather have a photo of Yuki than me on your phone, that's fine. Just don't expect me to be your girlfriend any more!'

Hiro looked sadly out of the window again. Where were they? He knew they'd left Belgium and were in Germany now because he'd seen a sign just before the last station. But what city came next? Was it Köln? In Köln, Hiro had to change trains. He wondered if he should ask the middle-aged woman sitting opposite. But just when he had decided not to, the train flew past a village and the woman suddenly spoke to him in English.

'Ha!' she said. 'There's my village! I'll be home in an hour. It's only ten minutes to Köln!'

Hiro smiled politely. The woman was a little bossy-looking and never seemed to sit still.

'But *you* are a long way from home ...' she went on. 'Are you Japanese?'

Hiro nodded. He didn't feel much like chatting, but it was clear the woman did. 'Yes,' he said, 'but I'm studying in England. I'm on a Study Year Abroad programme. This is my summer holiday.'

'Very good! And where are you going?' she went on.

'Berlin. I have an InterRail ticket,' Hiro answered, then seeing the confused look on her face, guessed he'd better explain. 'That means I can use my ticket to travel anywhere in Europe. Berlin is my first stop.'

'How exciting! But you're travelling alone. That's very brave.'

Hiro paused. 'My friends ...' he began. 'My friends ... couldn't come.'

'Oh, that's too bad,' the woman answered. She was about to say something else when her mobile phone rang. She searched excitedly in her bag, then began a loud conversation in German on her phone.

Hiro picked up his book. It was an American thriller – he'd brought it with him to practise his English – and with two violent murders already it was quite exciting. But Hiro couldn't read now. He thought sadly about what he'd just told the woman. It wasn't really the truth. The truth was that he and Akiko had planned to have a holiday together, but after their argument, everything had changed. They'd been so happy all the time they'd been together. She was on the same course in England and they'd met in the first week. And they'd never argued at all. So, then to get jealous about a dog! That was just crazy!

Hiro reached into his pocket and took out his own mobile phone. With one easy movement, he opened it and watched the screen come to life. For a moment or two he looked at his screensaver – the picture that appeared when he turned on his phone. It was a photo of Yuki, his beautiful twelve-year-old golden retriever, the most wonderful dog in the world. Then he chose 'My photos' from the menu on the side of the screen. Almost immediately, a picture of Akiko appeared. It was his favourite photo of her – the one at the restaurant where he'd taken her for her birthday. She looked so happy and so pretty! Hiro shook his head and quickly went back to the picture of the dog.

The argument had come out of nowhere. They'd been planning a beach holiday in southern Spain. When he'd invited his friends Ayumu and Daijiro and their girlfriends, Akiko had seemed happy enough. But then something had changed. He said he wished they could take Yuki as well, and all of a sudden Akiko had got angry. After that everything Hiro said seemed to make her angrier. She'd started talking about his screensaver, and the next thing he knew was she was shouting that she didn't want to see him ever again. It was just unbelievable. One moment he had a girlfriend, the next he didn't. Now, apparently, she'd gone off to Scotland with a couple of her friends. But he wasn't even sure of that. Their eight-month relationship had just exploded like a bomb.

All of a sudden Hiro realised a tear was running

down his cheek. Angrily, he brushed it away. The woman opposite was still talking loudly into her phone, so she hadn't seen the tear. But this was no way for a twenty-year-old Japanese man to behave. Hurriedly, he got out his InterRail map and pretended to study it closely. He'd left London that morning very early and taken the Eurostar to Brussels in Belgium. From there he'd caught this train going to Köln, and in Köln he would get the train to Berlin. But where would he go after that? Prague, the capital of the Czech Republic, was only five hours by train from Berlin. Then, he could go to Vienna, maybe. If there was time, he might even get to Budapest. How many new countries would he visit this trip? If he went to all those cities, it would make five!

Hiro began to feel more cheerful. He sat up and looked out of the window again at the countryside flying past. It seemed different and new all of a sudden. 'Yes,' Hiro thought, 'I will have an exciting and adventurous holiday. I'm not going to be sad. From this moment, Akiko is part of history. No more looking back; I will only look forward from now on.'

Chapter 2

A meeting with a shark

The train raced on for five minutes more, then began to slow down. The woman closed her phone and busily collected her things together.

'So, Köln!' she said brightly and stood up. 'Now I must find my husband and you must go to the Berlin train. Platform 2.'

Soon the train came to a stop and Hiro followed the woman off on to the platform. Immediately after they'd said goodbye, she called loudly to a tired-looking man waiting at the bottom of a staircase. The man hurried over to her, then followed her up the stairs, carrying all her bags.

Hiro made his way to Platform 2. He had half an hour to wait for his next train and, for some reason, sitting on the station made him feel lonely again. As soon as the train arrived, he climbed in. He found an empty seat, then sat looking out at the crowd of people outside the window. Hiro noticed an attractive blonde girl with a big blue bag getting on the train. He wondered if the girl might come and sit in the seat opposite him. But after taking a few steps towards him, she chose a seat three rows away. Hiro was disappointed.

Then a man with silvery-grey hair, wearing a grey raincoat got on. He was pulling a small suitcase on wheels. Hiro watched him come closer. He stopped some way down the train and spoke to one of the people there, giving a wide toothy smile. Hiro didn't like the look of the man. There was something about his smile, his grey clothes and the silent way he moved, which reminded Hiro of a shark. The man came down the train towards him. Hiro hoped the man would walk past. But he didn't.

'Excuse me,' the man said in English, giving the same smile. 'Is anyone sitting here?'

Hiro had no choice. As well as the seat beside him, the two opposite were free. 'No,' he said, 'of course ...'

'Thank you so much,' the man answered.

The man pushed his suitcase under the seat, then sat down opposite Hiro. Hiro felt uncomfortable. The man's eyes seemed very small and his teeth very sharp. Hiro was reminded of a shark once again.

He imagined the man swimming towards him and smiling. The smile made Hiro feel very cold, as if an icy hand had touched the back of his neck. He watched as the man took off his grey raincoat, took a mobile phone from the coat pocket and put the phone on the table between them. Hiro noticed the man's hands. They looked terribly clean and the fingernails perfect. Hiro wondered if the man might be a dentist.

The train pulled out of the station. Hiro tried to look away from the man and read his book again, but something kept making him look up. The man had taken a newspaper from his case and put on a pair of glasses now. He looked quite strong, but with his grey hair, Hiro guessed he must be in his mid-sixties, even seventy perhaps. After a while, the man put down the newspaper and checked his phone. He did everything very carefully, holding the phone at a distance, and looking at the screen. His fingers moved lightly over the keys. After a couple of minutes, the man put the phone onto the table, sat back in his seat and closed his eyes. Hiro suddenly felt much calmer. The man had made him nervous. It was like being near a dangerous animal. 'Yes,' Hiro decided, 'he's not a man; he's a shark.'

Hiro relaxed and read his book. The train was soon racing along again and his book was very exciting. The next time he checked his watch it was after four o'clock. He looked at the man opposite. 'Good, the Shark is still sleeping,' he thought.

Hiro got out his guidebook and tried to decide what to do when he reached Berlin. He had booked a room in a cheap hotel, the Hotel Alma, in an area called Kreuzberg. But how would he get there? There seemed to be an underground train called the U-Bahn, but also an overground one, the S-Bahn. Which one should he use?

All of a sudden, the train braked sharply and a number of things happened at once. The braking was so hard that a woman walking down the train fell across the table between Hiro and the Shark. As she fell, she knocked the Shark's newspaper and phone off the table and onto the seat beside Hiro. At the same moment the Shark jumped up and his hand shot out. But instead of helping the woman, he reached out across the table to try to get his things back. Hiro was very surprised. The Shark couldn't reach his things but, after a moment, he became quite pleasant again. Speaking in German, he took the woman's arm and helped her up. A conversation followed, then the woman went away.

The Shark sat down again. Almost immediately, he said, 'You have my mobile phone, I believe.'

Hiro didn't understand for a moment. Then he looked down at the seat beside him and saw the man's phone on his jacket. Hiro was surprised because he thought he'd put his own phone there. He picked up the phone and passed it across.

'I'm sorry,' he said.

'That's all right,' the Shark said, taking the phone. As he did so, their hands touched. The Shark's hand felt cold. 'These trains are so dangerous,' he went on. 'They are too fast! I am always nervous travelling in this country.'

'Yes,' Hiro answered.

'Will you excuse me for a moment?' the man said. 'Please be so kind to keep my seat for me.'

Without waiting for an answer, he picked up his phone and walked up the train to the toilet. Hiro watched the Shark close the toilet door, then saw the light above the door come on.

For a moment nothing happened, then Hiro heard the small ringing sound his phone made when a text message came through. He looked down. Under his jacket, he found his phone. So, it was there after all. His heart gave a tiny jump. Could it be a text from Akiko? He picked up the phone and pressed a key to open the message.

For a second or two he didn't understand. He could understand the English, but not what it meant. He read it twice.

MEET BRANDENBURG GATE 1PM TOMORROW. COLLECT EQUIPMENT AND HALF FEE.

It was another two or three seconds before Hiro realised the phone wasn't his.

Chapter 3
An amusing mistake

Hiro stared at the phone. Of course, he understood what had happened now – the Shark's phone was a Nokia just like his. In his excitement to check the message, Hiro hadn't noticed there was no screensaver, no photo of his dog.

Well, it was a simple mistake and there was nothing to feel guilty about. When the Shark returned from the toilet, Hiro would hand back the phone and apologise. The message didn't seem that private. Hiro knew the Brandenburg Gate was one of the most famous sights in Berlin. So, the man was meeting someone there. He was going to collect some equipment and half his fee. Surely there wasn't anything very private about that?

Hiro put the phone down and looked up. He wondered if the Shark had checked Hiro's phone and discovered the mistake, too. The light was still on above the toilet door. Perhaps even at this moment the Shark was reading one of the love messages Akiko had sent Hiro before their break-up. Hiro had saved seven or eight of them.

Hiro read the message on the Shark's phone once more. Perhaps it was the result of the book he was reading with all its murders, but the more Hiro looked at the message, the more uncomfortable he felt. There seemed to be something odd about it, something that wasn't quite right. He paused for a second, then did something really stupid. He knew it was stupid even before he did it, but it was just so easy. He pressed the Inbox key on the Shark's phone, and found the message list. The first message on the list – the one he'd just read – was from someone called 'M'. Hiro picked the next message. It was also from 'M'. Hiro looked up once more. It was safe: the toilet light was still on. He opened the message. The little screen filled immediately.

BERLIN ASSIGNMENT HOTEL ADLON ROOM 319 TUESDAY AFTER 8PM. HALF FEE AT MEETING, HALF ON COMPLETION.

Hiro wasn't sure he understood. His heart was beating fast. Part of the message was obvious: tomorrow was Tuesday and the Hotel Adlon must be in Berlin. He knew what a fee was, too: money that is paid for doing something. But what about the rest? Wasn't 'assignment' another word for 'job'? The word sounded a little bit odd. Wasn't 'assignment' a word a writer would use in a thriller to mean ...? No, that was a crazy thought! 'It must be the effect of that silly book I'm reading,' Hiro said to himself.

The next moment his heart stopped. When he looked up, the light above the toilet had gone out. Not only that, but the door was opening and the Shark was coming out. The old man was already making his way back towards him.

Hiro had to act fast. He closed the message, then dropped the phone back on to the seat beside him. Now he could relax: the Shark would never know Hiro had been reading the messages. Hiro watched the man come up.

A second later, Hiro realised his mistake. Of course the Shark would know! The last message had been received while he was in the toilet and Hiro had opened it then. It wouldn't show as a 'New Message' now, but as one that had been 'Read'. Hiro picked up the phone just as the Shark arrived.

Even before he sat down, the Shark spoke. 'Ha,

my friend!' he said with another toothy smile, 'I have just had a very amusing experience. When I was in the toilet, I decided to check the messages on my phone. But when I turned it on, I discovered—'

'I have your phone,' Hiro said quickly.

The Shark watched Hiro for a moment, then seemed to relax. Hiro had an odd feeling he'd spoken just in time.

'Yes,' he said, 'and I have yours. Is this your girlfriend?' he went on, giving a short laugh. 'She is very beautiful. What is her name?' The Shark held out Hiro's phone across the table. The screensaver photo of Yuki was showing.

'Yuki,' Hiro answered.

The Shark gave a strange nod of his head. 'A very beautiful dog. How amusing that we have the same kind of Nokia phone! Now perhaps you would return mine?'

Hiro was already holding the phone. He held it out, trying to stop his hand from shaking. 'I'm very sorry,' he said. 'A message came through and I opened it before I realised ...'

The Shark's eyes narrowed. He watched Hiro for a moment. 'Of course you did; that is quite natural,' he said, then looked at his phone. Hiro didn't move while the Shark opened the message. Hiro saw him read it, then close it again. 'Yes, from a business colleague,' the Shark said.

There was silence for a moment or two. Hiro didn't know what to say. Then the Shark slowly nodded his head and smiled. 'So, since we know each other's great secrets, I think we must introduce ourselves. My name is Erik Björnson. I am a businessman from Sweden. And who, may I ask, do I have the pleasure to meet?'

Chapter 4
A helping hand

Hiro felt hot. The train seemed to be travelling even faster.

'My name's Hiro Adachi,' he said. 'I'm from Japan.'

'Yes, of course,' the Shark answered. 'Japan is one of my favourite countries,' he went on. As he spoke, he sat forward, held out his hand and smiled. The smile seemed even more frightening than before.

'Pleased to meet you,' Hiro said, taking the man's hand. It felt cold and wet, like the skin of a fish.

'The pleasure is mine,' the Shark replied. 'So, I suppose you are a student taking a holiday?'

'Yes, I'm InterRailing,' replied Hiro.

'Very good. Berlin is your first stop?' the Shark asked.

'Yes,' said Hiro.

'And how many nights will you stay in Berlin? It is a very exciting city,' the Shark continued.

'I'm not sure,' Hiro answered.

The Shark nodded slowly. 'You have already booked a hotel, of course?'

Hiro had an uncomfortable feeling that there was a reason for the questions. He suddenly didn't want to tell the Shark where he was staying. 'Not yet. I was going to look around,' he replied. The Shark's eyes became very small.

'In Kreuzberg maybe,' Hiro added quickly. He wondered if that was enough information to give.

The Shark nodded. 'Perhaps I can suggest somewhere. The Hotel Modena? Cheap, but very comfortable.'

'Thank you so much. Maybe I'll try it,' replied Hiro.

'I shall telephone for you. The owner is an old friend,' the Shark said, reaching for his phone.

Hiro didn't know what to do. 'Thank you, but I'm hoping to meet someone in Kreuzberg ... a Japanese friend ... from my city,' he said weakly.

There was silence for a moment. It was a lie and Hiro could see the Shark knew it. Hiro felt very hot.

The Shark smiled. 'Of course. It was simply an idea.' He watched Hiro thoughtfully for a few moments, then spoke again. 'I must apologise to you, my friend. There is something terrible I must tell you. I am a very stupid old man. I read some messages on your phone before I understood it was not mine. I imagine you did the same?'

Hiro felt a drop of sweat run out of his hair. The lights in the train suddenly seemed very bright. 'No,' he said. 'Only one. About your meeting at the Brandenburg Gate.'

There was a long silence again. Hiro wanted to brush the sweat from his forehead. The silence seemed to go on forever. Finally, the man gave another smile and looked away.

* * *

At Hannover the train was delayed for half an hour, so it was after seven thirty when they reached Berlin. It was a rainy evening and already getting dark, so the lights of the city shone all around. Hiro felt more relaxed. For the rest of the journey the Shark had slept – well, he'd had his eyes closed. Hiro couldn't be certain he was asleep. Hiro felt silly now for thinking so badly of the old man. Obviously, Hiro's imagination had gone wild after reading that thriller. After all, the man was old enough to be his grandfather – how could anyone like that be dangerous?

Finally they pulled into the station, a huge modern building. Hiro picked up his bag and stood up. Although he felt better, he wanted to get away from the old man as quickly as possible.

'It was very nice to meet you,' Hiro said politely.

The Shark also got up. 'How will you get to Kreuzberg?' he asked.

'I'm going to take the U-Bahn,' Hiro said.

'No, no, that is not good. I shall show you the best way.'

Hiro's heart raced. 'It's very kind of you, but I'll be fine.'

The Shark took Hiro's arm. 'It is no problem.'

Hiro felt the Shark's hand lead him forward, off the train. The platform was busy, but Hiro suddenly felt very alone. Even though he'd persuaded himself that his fears were just the result of a stupid book, Hiro realised he was shaking a little. Here he was in a foreign city, where he didn't speak the language, and this old man was making him afraid.

'Follow me,' the Shark said. 'I will take you to the S-Bahn, to the correct platform, then leave you there.'

Hiro knew he couldn't argue. He tried to keep calm. 'This will be all right,' he told himself. 'In five minutes I'll be on my own again.'

The Shark led the way along the platform until they came to an escalator going down. 'You must take the S-Bahn to Friedrichstrasse,' he said as they stepped together on to the moving escalator. 'It is the next stop. Then you will take the U-Bahn to Hallesches Tor in Kreuzberg. Do you understand?'

The Shark's face was close to Hiro's; his teeth were bright in the station lights.

'Thank you. Yes,' Hiro replied.

They walked across a wide hall. A family of Japanese were standing under a big clock. Hiro thought of calling out to them for help, but couldn't think what to say. A moment later he had passed them and it was too late in any case.

They reached another escalator. This time they went up. The Shark didn't speak. Hiro told himself, 'Only another couple of minutes, then I'll be safe.'

They came out onto another platform. It was wide, but quite crowded near the escalator.

'Come, there is more room further down,' the Shark said.

'I'll be fine now, thank you,' Hiro said.

'No, I shall wait,' the Shark answered. 'I must be sure you take the correct train.'

They stopped two thirds of the way along the platform. It was less wide just there because of a large seat. They were standing quite close to the edge. The sound of a train made Hiro turn around. It was coming in fast. He saw the lights on the front, the driver looking out. Hiro felt the Shark move in closer to him.

The next moment Hiro had a sudden idea of what might happen. Everyone on the platform was looking forward, watching the train. No one was looking in their direction. The Shark was going to push him. He was going to push him off the platform in front of the train!

At the last second Hiro moved back from the edge of the platform. At the same time the Shark seemed to reach out as if he was falling. Hiro felt the Shark take his arm, but Hiro was now away from the danger. The next moment the train had raced past. The scream of brakes followed. A few seconds later the train had come to a stop.

Chapter 5
A difficult decision

'Please! You frightened me! You nearly fell!' the Shark said.

Hiro stared in fear, unable to speak. The old man's face was close to Hiro's and he was holding his arm very tightly.

'You must not stand so close to the edge of the platform!' the Shark went on. 'But this is your train. Climb in quickly!' He moved even closer to Hiro. 'Take great care, young man. Leave Berlin alive – not in a coffin!'

Their eyes met for a second, then Hiro felt the Shark give him a push. A moment later Hiro found himself inside the train, the electric doors closing behind him.

Almost immediately the train began to pull out of the station. Hiro couldn't move. He stood in the doorway, looking at the Shark outside on the platform. The old man didn't move either, but watched Hiro all the time as the train pulled away. Then the train left the bright lights of the station and the Shark disappeared from view.

At last Hiro was alone. Without thinking, he fell into a seat. Suddenly he realised he was wet with sweat. He undid his jacket. Was he dreaming or had the Shark really tried to kill him? It seemed a completely crazy idea, but Hiro couldn't think of any other explanation. The Shark had led him to the edge of the platform, he'd moved behind Hiro, then reached out and caught his arm. And what was that final thing he'd said? 'Leave Berlin alive – not in a coffin!' Wasn't a coffin the wooden box they use for dead bodies? Hiro suddenly felt very cold. He stared out through the train window at the city, but saw nothing except the Shark's cold grey eyes looking back at him.

How he reached his hotel that night, Hiro never knew. It was like a terrible dream. When he thought about it later, he had a memory of getting off the train at Friedrichstrasse and following a group of other travellers down into the U-Bahn. He couldn't remember anything of that underground journey except hearing 'Hallesches Tor!' After that he somehow made his way through the streets in the darkness, following the map in his guidebook. But he remembered the little old man,

Herr Albert, who opened the door of the Hotel Alma when Hiro pressed the bell. Herr Albert had taken Hiro up to the second floor in an old lift with metal gates and wooden doors. That evening the hotel seemed like a second home to Hiro and Herr Albert like a second father. Hiro fell into bed and was asleep only a few seconds later.

* * *

When Hiro woke the next morning, everything came back to him immediately. There seemed to be no escape from the awful dream. The moment he opened his eyes, it felt as if the Shark was standing next to the bed and whispering, 'Leave Berlin alive – not in a coffin!'

Hiro's first idea was to catch the earliest train out of the city. He would go directly to Prague, or maybe Warsaw or Amsterdam – anywhere as long as he could get out of Berlin.

But then, as Hiro lay in bed looking up at the ceiling, thinking about what had happened on the platform, he started to feel angry. 'Why should an old man make me run off?' he thought. Hiro began to wonder why he'd been so afraid. Perhaps it was because he was safe inside his hotel room, but Hiro thought he should teach the Shark a lesson. He would show him who was boss!

Hiro felt confused, but the longer he lay there, the angrier he became. If the Shark had really tried to push him off the platform, then that was ... Hiro sat up, his blood boiling. Who was this man who called himself Erik Björnson? If he had really wanted to kill Hiro, it must be because of the messages Hiro had read on his phone. There was one idea that Hiro couldn't get out of his mind – the Shark was a killer. And the messages meant that he was planning to kill someone that night. Hiro had to do something. But what?

He thought about Akiko. She always knew what to do. For a moment he considered phoning her, but then he stopped himself. No, when Akiko had said she didn't want to hear from him, he'd replied, 'Don't worry, you won't!' He wouldn't be the weak one. If she decided to phone him, well, that was different. Hiro jumped up from the bed, angry that he'd even considered the idea for a second.

When Hiro went into breakfast, Herr Albert gave him a friendly wave and took him to a table. At one table a young American couple were discussing a boat trip on the Wannsee. Hiro ate some cereal, thinking how good it would be to have such an uncomplicated stay in the city. All of a sudden he realised that Herr Albert was at his shoulder.

'You would like an egg?' Herr Albert was asking softly.

'I'm sorry,' Hiro answered. 'No, no egg, thank you.' Then, without knowing he was about to say it, he went on, 'Could you tell me where the nearest police station is?'

Chapter 6 A visit to the police station

Half an hour later, Hiro was outside the police station at Hallesches Tor. Looking up at the building he felt his new confidence suddenly leave him. It was a huge grey place with very few windows and, standing there, Hiro began to feel nervous. He thought about the lie he had told Herr Albert – that his camera had been stolen and he wanted to report it. How he wished that was true. How he wished that he had never met the Shark and that all he had to worry about was a missing camera. Suddenly it seemed like a big mistake to come to the police. He wasn't even certain any more that the Shark had tried to kill him.

From the start it didn't go well. The first police officer he spoke to could understand very little English, and immediately called for someone else. Hiro waited nervously for half an hour in the crowded waiting room, watching people come and go.

At last, a woman police officer in a bright green and white uniform appeared. She introduced herself as Petra Müller, and led Hiro off to a small glass-walled office at the back of the police station.

Hiro began badly. 'I think an old man tried to kill me,' he said. At that, the police officer raised her eyebrows. 'I read some messages on this man's phone. I think he's going to murder someone tonight in the Hotel Adlon,' Hiro continued. 'And then he tried to push me off the platform in front of a train.' The words came falling out of Hiro's mouth. Within half a minute, he was in a terrible mess.

'All right,' the police officer said quietly. 'Perhaps we should take this a bit more slowly.' Hiro had to repeat himself while the police officer took several pages of notes. Then she finally stood up and told Hiro she was going to get someone else.

It was half an hour before she reappeared, this time with an older man, who was fat and smelt strongly of cigarettes. He wasn't wearing a uniform and Hiro decided he must be a detective. The detective didn't introduce himself. He sat on the table and crossed his arms.

'So, you're the Japanese boy who thinks an old man has tried to kill him. Is that correct?' the detective started.

Hiro didn't know how to answer.

'Is that correct?' the detective repeated.

'Yes, that's right,' Hiro said at last.

'And why do you believe this old man wished to murder you?' the detective asked.

Hiro felt more nervous all the time. 'I explained to your colleague that—'

'I don't wish to know what you explained to my colleague. I want you to tell me!' the detective said angrily. Hiro looked up at the detective. He seemed to be in a very bad mood – as if he would start shouting at any moment.

'By accident I read some messages on the old man's phone,' Hiro said quietly. 'We were on the train and I picked up his phone by mistake.'

'Yes, yes, I know all that,' the detective said impatiently. 'What I want to know is why you believe an old man would wish to kill you for that!'

Hiro smelt cigarettes on the detective's breath again. 'I think the messages I read on the old man's phone were very important,' Hiro said quietly. 'One message said he had an assignment at the Hotel Adlon.'

The detective's eyes lit up. 'Ah, an assignment!' He smiled at the woman police officer. 'I'm sorry. Go on.'

Hiro felt hot. 'And the other message said he was

going to collect half his fee and some equipment today at—'

'Equipment, eh!' the detective broke in. 'And what do you think is meant by that?'

'I'm not sure,' Hiro said nervously. 'I thought ...' Hiro came to a stop.

'Well?' the detective said.

'I'm not sure,' Hiro answered. 'I thought it might be a gun,' he said at last, dropping his head.

There was silence. Hiro could feel the detective's eyes on him. Finally, the man got up from the table and began to walk round the room. 'OK, let's leave all that for the moment. Now, you say he tried to kill you. How exactly did he do that?'

'We were on the platform at the main station,' Hiro explained. 'He was standing behind me. I think he was going to push me.'

'You *think* he was going to push you.' The detective said the words slowly.

'Yes, and he got hold of my arm,' Hiro went on.

'And he got hold of your arm,' the detective repeated after him.

There was silence. Hiro felt his face going red. Now that he'd said out loud what he believed, it suddenly seemed very stupid. He saw the detective watching him. The man just gave a tired nod. Then he spoke.

'I guess you like spy films, yes? James Bond, Jason Bourne, this sort of rubbish?'

Hiro didn't look up.

'You know, I suppose, that it's a very serious business to waste police time,' the detective went on.

'Yes, I do,' Hiro answered.

'And you can imagine how busy we are,' the detective said.

Hiro nodded. There was silence again.

The detective went on at last. 'What are you doing here in Berlin alone?'

'I'm on an InterRail trip,' Hiro replied.

'I know. But why are you by yourself? Where are your friends?' the detective asked.

'I ... I was going to have a holiday with my girlfriend, but ... we've just broken up,' Hiro said quietly.

'Ah! So now we have it. A broken heart!' The detective shook his head and walked over to the door. 'Look, my friend,' he said, 'Nobody is trying to kill you, and there aren't going to be any murders in the Hotel Adlon tonight. You're living in a dream. You see one thing and you imagine another. It's all in your mind. Now, return to your hotel, pack your bags and get a train back to England as fast as you can. Buy your girlfriend some flowers, that's my advice.'

With that, he hurried out of the door, calling some orders in German to the woman police officer as he left the room.

Hiro looked down at the floor. He had never before felt so small.

Chapter 7
Painful thoughts

When Hiro got back to his hotel, he went to his room, lay down on the bed and didn't move for a long time.

He felt terrible. The police hadn't believed him. Worse than that, they'd made him feel like a schoolboy again, a schoolboy who dreamt of spy stories and cried over the girlfriend he'd lost.

The visit to the police station made him remember something that had happened when he was about thirteen. It wasn't a happy memory. One very snowy day on his way to school, Hiro saw a man breaking the side window of a car. The man got in and drove off. Hiro quickly wrote down the number of the car, then called 110, the emergency number of the police. All day Hiro felt very proud of what he'd done and told all his school friends. But that evening Hiro's father took a call from the police. The man who had 'stolen' the car was its owner. The locks on the car had frozen and he'd needed his car in an emergency. Hiro felt very stupid and never told any of his friends the end of the story.

Now he had the same feeling. What had the detective said about seeing one thing and imagining another? Hiro wouldn't tell anyone about his visit to the police that morning and he would never again ask them for help.

After half an hour of such thoughts, Hiro suddenly jumped up from the bed. Lying there like that, reliving the past and feeling sorry for himself, was weak. That was schoolboy behaviour – just like keeping all those love messages from Akiko on his phone. Immediately, he picked up his phone, went to Akiko's texts, and prepared to delete them. His hand shook for a second or two. 'Delete all messages?' appeared on the screen. With a little cry of pain, he pressed the 'OK' key.

After that, Hiro put on his jacket and hurried out of his room, almost knocking over Herr Albert, who was cleaning the corridor. He went down in the old wooden lift and quickly out into the street. He had no idea where he was going or what he was going to do, but the sun was shining now. He tried to tell himself he was happier.

He stopped in a small café a short way up the road, and asked for a green tea. He took his cup and went to sit by the window. Looking out, watching all the people passing, his head began to feel clearer. He tried to decide what to do. As he was on holiday, Hiro thought he really ought to do some sightseeing. He took out his guidebook and started to read.

The very first place he found, on the first page of the guidebook, was the Brandenburg Gate. Hiro stared at the picture. The words seemed to jump out of the page at him: 'The Brandenburg Gate, Berlin's most famous sight, is in Pariser Platz, where the famous Hotel Adlon can also be found.' The Brandenburg Gate ... the Hotel Adlon. Hiro read the words again, then looked at his watch. It was twelve o'clock. In one hour the Shark would be at his meeting; he would collect the gun and get the first half of his fee.

Hiro had a sick feeling in his stomach. His heart had started to beat very fast. He closed his eyes. When he opened them again, he knew what he must do. He'd found the strength to delete Akiko's messages; now he had to be brave again. If the police wouldn't go to the Brandenburg Gate, he would have to do it himself. There was just time to get there before one o'clock.

Immediately, he pushed his tea away and hurried across the café. He almost threw a five-euro note across the counter. He didn't wait for any change.

There wasn't a moment to lose.

He found a U-Bahn station just round the corner and stopped at the map inside the entrance. Which was the way to go? He needed to get to Unter den Linden – that was the nearest stop to the Brandenburg Gate. It seemed very complicated: he would have to travel up to Friedrichstrasse and then get a different line. Remembering what his guidebook said, he hurried into a newspaper shop to buy a train ticket, then ran down to the platform.

At least he didn't have to wait long. Soon a train arrived and he jumped in. He went to stand against the opposite door, too nervous and excited to sit down.

The journey seemed endless, although it wasn't more than five stops. Then he was running along the platform and up and down the stairs to get to the other line.

This time there was a longer wait. He had just missed a train. It was already 12:40 – only twenty minutes before the Shark's meeting. Hiro walked up and down the platform.

At 12:45 the train appeared at last. The moment it stopped Hiro opened the door and jumped inside. It was only one stop now, three or four minutes, no more. He tried to calm himself down, take some deep breaths. The train pulled out of the station and raced into the darkness. Surely now he must be there in time?

Chapter 8
A little bit of sightseeing

When Hiro came out of the underground station five minutes later, he found himself in a wide street. Smart shops and hotels stretched away in both directions – and there was the Brandenburg Gate, a couple of hundred metres away. Hiro saw the six columns of the great Greek-style gateway, just as he'd seen in the guidebook, and on its top, the horses and chariot against the sky.

Hiro made his way towards the Gate. It was 12:50. Now he had to take great care. He would have to get close to the Gate if he wanted to see the Shark's meeting take place. But he also had to make sure he kept out of sight. He must make sure the Shark didn't see him.

At first there was no problem. Cars were parked all the way up the street and Hiro kept close to these. On the left-hand side he noticed the entrance to the Hotel Adlon, a grand building with a revolving door. If Hiro was right, it was there that evening the Shark would complete his work.

Further up the street it became more difficult. The street opened up into a wide square – the Pariser Platz. Now Hiro could be seen more easily. But there were plenty of cars here too, many of them very large, with dark windows. He walked past these, getting closer all the time to the Gate. Now he could see how big it was. There were lots of people wandering about around the columns. He didn't know what to do. Perhaps the Shark would meet his friend on the other side of the Gate, where most of the tourists were. But to get close was so dangerous! It was 12:55. If only he weren't so easy to notice. If only he weren't Japanese!

A coach pulling up on the far side of the Gate caught his eye. After a few moments, the passengers came pouring out of its door. Hiro had an idea. The tourists were all Europeans or Americans, but if he could get round to that side, a coach full of Japanese tourists was sure to appear soon. He began to make his way round.

Hiro was nearly there, when just as he'd guessed, a coach pulled up by the side of the road. Almost immediately thirty or forty Japanese tourists of all ages came hurrying down the steps. Hiro went to join them.

The sound of his own language made him want to cry out, but he stopped himself. He had to look out for the Shark. Several of the group hurried forward, pulling cameras from cases, and Hiro moved with them. As he got nearer the Gate, his eyes searched the foot of the columns. He couldn't see the Shark. He looked at his watch. It was exactly one o'clock.

Hiro studied the people round the Gate. Several were wandering around, looking up at the columns or standing for photographs, but none of them looked anything like the Shark. The only person over fifty years old was a priest, wearing long black clothes, standing away to the left. Hiro felt disappointed. After fighting his fears so bravely, was it all for nothing? Hiro watched as the priest was joined by a second man. The two of them went off behind one of the columns and disappeared from view.

Five minutes passed. Hiro began to wonder if he'd made a mistake. Should he go back to the other side of the Gate?

An old man walking with a stick came slowly past. Hiro's heart missed a beat. He couldn't see the man's face. Was this the Shark, pretending to need a stick? Hiro moved in order to see the man's face, but then stopped. A little old woman, perhaps eighty years of age, had joined the old man.

Hiro shook his head and looked at his watch: 1:10. Was the Shark really not coming? Hiro began to consider the possibilities. What if, following the mix-up with the phones, the Shark had changed the time or place of the meeting?

A hand on his shoulder made Hiro jump. For a second he thought it must be the Shark. Then he gave a sick laugh. One of the Japanese women from the coach was smiling at him and holding out her camera. She wanted Hiro to take a photo of her and her friend in front of the Gate, and she was speaking in Japanese. Hiro felt stupid – he'd been in such a dream that he hadn't even recognised his own language. He took the photo as asked, handed back the camera, and looked at his watch. It was 1:20.

So, the Shark wasn't coming after all. Hiro felt very stupid. 'Perhaps the detective at the police station was right,' he thought. 'Perhaps I should just take the first train back to England.' He walked straight towards the Gate, no longer hiding among the Japanese tourists, and headed for the underground station. He just wanted to get out of

Berlin now, to get out of this stupid city.

Hiro was less than fifty metres from the underground station, when the sound of a car close behind him made him look round. A black BMW with dark windows stopped beside him. As it did so, the back window opened and a dark-haired man looked out.

'Mr Hiro Adachi?' the man asked in English. He didn't wait for an answer. 'I'd like a word with you. It's very important.'

Chapter 9
The safe house

Hiro looked inside the car. 'Yes?' he said. He was too surprised to say anything else.

'My name is Karl Meier,' the man went on. He was very smartly dressed. 'I work for the *Bundesnachrichtendienst*. The BND is a department of the German police. Foreign intelligence. We need to talk to you. Get in, please.'

At the same moment the driver of the car climbed out. His head was shaved and he wore a black leather jacket. He looked very tough. He opened the back door for Hiro.

Hiro felt his heart beat fast. 'Yes, of course,' he said. He was feeling very nervous, not sure if he should get in, but the driver put his hand on Hiro's shoulder. Hiro climbed into the car next to Karl Meier. Almost immediately, the driver banged the door shut, got in the front and the car pulled away. It had all happened so quickly, Hiro couldn't think.

'Don't worry, my friend,' Meier said. 'You're quite safe with us.' He put out his hand. 'I'm very pleased to meet you, Mr Adachi. You're a very brave young man.'

Hiro shook the man's hand. The car had already left Unter den Linden and was racing through the streets. Hiro saw the driver watching him in the mirror. He had a long cut on his face.

'Where are we going?' Hiro asked Karl Meier.

'Just somewhere we can talk more quietly, Mr Adachi.' The man gave a strange smile. In the car mirror, Hiro saw the driver smile, too. Hiro began to feel uncomfortable. How could the police have known where he was? He wished he hadn't got into the car now. Why hadn't one of the men shown him a police card or something?

The car raced on. No one spoke. Hiro had no idea where they were.

At last Hiro managed to find his voice. 'How did you know where to find me?' he said with a cough.

Meier didn't look at him. 'We've been following you for some time,' he said quietly.

Hiro saw the driver smile once again.

'You mean since I went to the police station this morning?' Hiro asked.

Meier looked round at that. He watched Hiro for a moment or two, then nodded very gently. 'Yes, that's right. There are some things you said which we want to double-check.'

Hiro did his best to relax. At least he had an explanation now for how they'd picked him up.

At last they turned into a small street and drove round to the back of a large building. Hiro wasn't sure if it was offices or flats. Then the car pulled over the pavement and went down into an underground car park. The car headlights shone brightly in the darkness. Hiro felt a little sick.

They came to a stop opposite a lift. Immediately, the driver got out and told Hiro to follow him. Hiro climbed out of the car and a moment later, Meier joined them.

'This is what we call a "safe house",' Meier said. 'We use it for interviews, among other things. Naturally, we can't take most people to our head office. Please follow me.'

Meier led the way over to the lift, pressed a button on the wall and the doors opened immediately. The three of them went inside. It was dirty and smelly. An empty beer can was lying on the floor. With a tired look, Meier kicked it away.

The lift went slowly up, then the doors opened.

When they stepped out there were two brown doors in front of them, a long corridor leading off to the right, and stairs up and down.

The driver took a key from his pocket, and unlocked the door on the left, then Meier led the way inside. Hiro relaxed a little when he saw it was a simple flat. There was a bedroom and bathroom off to one side of the hall, a kitchen directly ahead and a lounge to the right. They went into the lounge and Meier turned on the light. There was very little furniture: a sofa and two armchairs, a coffee table, a TV, but it seemed no one lived there. There were no pictures on the wall, and there was nothing very warm about the room. Meier sat in one of the armchairs.

'Please have a seat,' he said, pointing to the sofa. 'Would you like a coffee, perhaps?' he added.

'No, thank you,' Hiro answered.

Meier spoke quickly in German to the driver, who went off into the kitchen. Hiro didn't like the feeling in the room. It was cold and strange.

Meier seemed in a hurry to start. 'So, when you went to the police this morning, the ordinary police, that is—'

'I thought they hadn't believed me,' Hiro broke in.

Meier's eyes narrowed. 'Yes, you're right. They're very stupid people. The truth is that your report was picked up on our computer. We acted immediately.'

'I see,' Hiro answered, a little uncertainly.

Meier looked uncomfortable. 'Right, now it's important that you tell me in your own words what you told the ordinary police. You told them about the old man on the train, of course. And what did you tell them about the messages that you read on his phone?' Meier was sitting forward now and looking very closely at Hiro. Hiro didn't answer. This is all wrong, he thought. The men are wrong, the room is wrong, the questions are wrong. He didn't know what to do.

'So?' said Meier impatiently.

Hiro looked at the man. 'I'm sorry. Is there a toilet I could use, please?'

Meier looked annoyed for a moment, then seemed to relax. 'Yes, of course,' he said with a smile. 'I'll show you.'

'Thank you,' Hiro replied.

Meier led Hiro out of the room and opened the bathroom door for him. Hiro went in and closed the door. He heard Meier go off into the kitchen and start talking to the driver. Hiro sat on the edge of the bath and put his head in his hands. He had to think. 'These men aren't real policemen, or foreign intelligence,' he said to himself. 'They must be friends of the Shark. Perhaps they followed me from the Brandenburg Gate. Yes, that must be it! Maybe the Shark *had* been at the Gate earlier. He'd met these men there. When they saw me, they decided to follow me and pick me up. So what are they going to do with me now?'

Hiro looked around. He had to escape. There was no way out of the bathroom except through the door. What could he do?

He got up, went over to the door and listened. He could hear Meier talking in German. It sounded as though he had returned to the lounge. Maybe he was talking on the phone.

Hiro's brain was racing. He thought: 'They want to be sure what I know.' That was why Meier was asking the questions and not the Shark – by pretending to be police they hoped to get more information from him. If the Shark asked the questions, Hiro might refuse to talk. But once they'd heard everything, surely they would kill him. 'It'll be a shot in the back of the head,' Hiro told himself. 'Either that, or a fall from the window, perhaps.'

There was no time to think about it any more. Hiro looked round the bathroom once more. Then he made a decision. He had one chance only. If he was going to escape, it had to be now.

He stood by the door.

Chapter 10
Escape!

Very carefully, Hiro opened the bathroom door and put his head out into the hall. He'd been right – Meier was back in the lounge. He was talking on his phone, looking down, deep in conversation. The driver was out of sight in the kitchen.

Hiro took a deep breath. He had only a few seconds to get to the front door. He took off his shoes and quietly crossed the hall. Five steps only and he was at the front door. If the door was locked, he was finished ...

He was in luck. With a tiny sound, the door opened, then he was out into the main corridor. He ran straight to the stairs.

He went down only three or four steps before he realised he was making a mistake. 'No,' he thought. 'Once they realise I've gone, they'll expect me to go down, so I must go up instead.' He turned and ran back up the steps two at a time. He'd just managed to reach the next floor when he heard the men run out of the flat, shouting in German. He heard them stop outside the lift.

Hiro could only guess what they were shouting, but then he heard their footsteps hurrying down the stairs.

So, what to do now? Hiro's heart was racing. In a short time the men would realise he hadn't gone down and they would fly back up the steps. A fire escape! There had to be a fire escape in a place like this. But where?

He ran up two floors without stopping, still carrying his shoes. Then he was at the top – there were no more stairs, just another corridor. Far below he could hear the men shouting. Then silence. They were listening for him. Listening for his footsteps. Then Hiro heard one of them coming up.

There was nothing for it. Hiro ran the length of the corridor. At the end of the corridor there was a door. He pushed and the door opened.

Hiro found himself outside on a fire escape, a metal staircase going down the outside of the building. Should he go down? He had no choice. At any moment the man coming up would look along the corridor and see him.

Hiro went down a couple of steps, then heard a door opening somewhere below. He ran back up and watched as the driver came out on to the fire escape two floors below him. Hiro saw him look down, then, just as the man was about to look up, Hiro pressed himself back against the wall. His heart was beating crazily. Surely the man would see him! Two or three seconds passed. Then Hiro heard the man shout back into the building before he went inside and the door banged shut. Hiro took another deep breath. He was out of danger!

Hiro was just about to start down the steps, when something stopped him again. Was it a tiny sound from below or something else? The memory of something from a film came back to him. It had been a trick! The driver's shout had been a trick to make Hiro think the way was safe – the man had closed the door loudly, but he was still outside on the fire escape at that moment, looking up. Hiro didn't move. He closed his eyes. Akiko's face came to his mind. 'Please help me,' he said softly. Ten long seconds passed, then there was a quiet call from below. After that the door closed again. This time Hiro knew the man had really gone inside.

Hiro's legs were shaking as he made his way down the stairs. He didn't stop now or look around. The only thing he thought about was getting to the bottom. He almost fell once, but managed to stop himself, then in thirty seconds he was down on the ground.

He found himself on a small path between buildings. One way led to the main street at the front of the building. He could see people walking past. That was the way to go. Hiro walked quickly towards the street. Just as he got there, he saw a bus pull up about ten metres down the road. He didn't stop to think, but ran towards it. He reached the bus just as the driver was about to close the doors. Hiro almost threw himself inside and fell on to a seat.

As the bus pulled away, Hiro saw Meier appear through the glass door of the building he'd just left. Hiro dropped his head from view, pretending to tie up his shoes. It was another couple of minutes before he was brave enough to raise his head and look around. When he did, he took out his phone and opened his photo of Akiko. '*Arigato*,' he whispered. 'Thank you.' Then, under his breath, 'I'm so sorry I deleted your messages. It was a terrible mistake.'

Chapter 11

The eye of the storm

Ten minutes later the bus pulled into a huge modern square and stopped. Most of the passengers hurried off. Not wanting to be alone anywhere now, Hiro followed them. He felt safer where there were crowds of people, and this place was busy with shoppers. Even so, he couldn't stop himself looking back every ten seconds or so. Had Meier seen him take the bus and guessed where it was going?

To one side of the square there was a wall where a number of people were sitting. There was a kebab-seller nearby and most of the people on the wall were eating snacks. They looked relaxed and cheerful, chatting and taking photographs of one another. Hiro went over and sat down in the middle of them. Being Japanese he knew he could be easily noticed, but with so many people around surely he wasn't in danger.

Once he'd sat down, Hiro realised how terribly tired he was. His first thought was to return to his hotel and just fall on the bed. It would be so wonderful to sleep again untroubledly. He felt as though he'd been living in fear of his life for weeks. Was it really only twenty-four hours since he met the Shark?

A cinema sign on the far side of the square caught Hiro's eye. All of a sudden the idea of sitting in the darkness, safe from the world for a couple of hours, seemed wonderful. It would be like the calm time in the middle of the storm. What did they call it – the eye? Without wasting another moment, he got up and hurried over to the cinema entrance. He couldn't stop himself from looking behind as he went, but no one appeared to be following him.

When he arrived at the box office, he discovered he was in luck. A new thriller was about to start. He paid, bought a hotdog and went through to find a seat.

Some advertisements were showing when he went in, but it was beautifully dark. Still worried that someone may be following him, he chose a seat right at the back. In that way, he thought, he could see everyone who entered. He sat down and immediately began eating the hotdog. He hadn't thought about food since breakfast and was surprised to find how hungry he was.

Very soon the film started. Thankfully, it was in English and not German. All the same, it made Hiro feel exhausted; everyone spoke very quickly and Hiro found it hard to follow. He started thinking about what had happened that day. He had to find the answers to some questions.

Hiro was absolutely certain now that the Shark was an assassin – a professional killer. The old man had come to Berlin to kill someone. The text message had said, 'Berlin Assignment Hotel Adlon Room 319 Tuesday after 8pm', so the murder was to take place that evening in Room 319 of the Hotel Adlon. He supposed the Shark had been at the Brandenburg Gate after all, probably with Meier. When they saw Hiro there, they'd decided Meier would follow him. They wanted to know if the police knew about the Hotel Adlon. If they did, then the Shark might have to cancel his plan. Yes, that must be it! So what about the murder? Would it still go ahead? And what should Hiro do?

Hiro felt so tired thinking about all these questions and worrying about what to do. It seemed to him that the trip had become some kind of test. He remembered something his grandfather had said to him, shortly before he died. The old man was very ill and had only a few days to live, so the whole family had come to say goodbye. Taking Hiro by the arm, the old man had pulled Hiro close to the bed. 'Life is an examination, Hiro-chan,' he said. 'Make me proud.' Those words rang in Hiro's ears now. Is this what the old man meant? Hiro shook his head, exhausted, and closed his eyes. The film music washed over him like waves on the beach.

The next thing Hiro knew, a man in a white shirt and black tie had his arm on Hiro's shoulder. The man was shaking him hard. The man said something in German, then tried in English: 'Hey! No sleeping here!'

Hiro shook his head. 'What?' he said. He couldn't understand where he was. Then he remembered.

'No sleeping!' The man in the white shirt was still shaking him. 'Go to a hotel if you want to sleep!'

Hiro pulled himself up. 'I'm sorry.'

The man gave an angry look, but moved away, collecting rubbish from the seats.

Hiro looked at his watch: 5:45! He couldn't believe it. He must have slept through the rest of the film.

He got to his feet. Then the full memory of the last twenty-four hours hit him: the Shark ... the Brandenburg Gate ... Meier and the safe house ...

Hiro fell back in the seat and put his hands to his head.

Chapter 12
A voice in the ear

It was almost six o'clock when Hiro left the cinema. There were dark clouds in the sky and all around the square the lights from advertisements shone as brightly as if it were night. For a moment Hiro thought he could be back in Tokyo. It made him feel terribly homesick. But he wasn't at home. A sign above the cinema read: 'Alexanderplatz'. He looked at the map in his guidebook to see where he was.

Alexanderplatz wasn't difficult to find on the map. He saw he wasn't very far from his hotel – only seven or eight stops on the U-Bahn. Without thinking, Hiro walked towards the U-Bahn entrance. He didn't have much idea what he was going to do when he got back to his hotel room. He supposed he was just going to lie on the bed and read or watch TV until he was able to sleep. Then he would leave Berlin the following morning. His trip seemed a failure, but he'd had enough. He felt frightened and tired and cold. Hadn't he done all he could? He'd been brave and put himself in danger – his grandfather couldn't be disappointed with him. Why shouldn't Hiro just quietly leave Berlin now and go somewhere else?

Alexanderplatz station was big and busy. There seemed to be several lines, both overground and underground – he checked the map again and chose U-Bahn 2. He would have to change trains once.

He didn't have to wait long for a train. He climbed in and sat in the corner. The train was very full. Looking up and down he watched all the different men and women, old and young, rich and poor. Some were clearly on their way home from work, others were just starting out for the evening. He watched a couple of his age, talking closely together and sharing a quick kiss. How wonderful, he thought. How lovely it must be to have so few cares in the world. The stations hurried by one after another. Dreamily, Hiro watched the lively city passing before his eyes.

It was only when they pulled into Potsdamer Platz that Hiro realised he'd missed his station. Looking at the map on the inside of the train he saw that he had forgotten to get out earlier and change to U-Bahn 6. With a shake of his head, he jumped up and went to the door.

Just before stepping out of the train, he stopped. 'Why shouldn't I just continue the journey?' he thought. 'I could go on to the end of the line and get the train back. It would at least kill some time.'

With a smile he went back to his seat. The woman sitting in the next seat seemed surprised. The train pulled out. Hiro looked at his watch: 6:35. He tried to relax.

Five minutes later he knew it was impossible. He couldn't sit still. He couldn't simply go back to his hotel and pretend he knew nothing of the Shark's plans. A voice was whispering in his ear. The voice had started the moment Hiro had decided to go back to his hotel room. 'Coward!' it was saying. 'You're not brave at all. You're being a coward!'

With each station that passed the feeling grew worse. He looked at his watch again. It was 6:45 now. It hit him then – in about an hour's time it was quite possible that a murder would take place! Hiro began to feel very sick. He was the only person who knew about the Shark's plans. He was the only person who might stop them. He had to go back. He had to do something. When the train pulled into the next station, Hiro was already waiting at the door to go back.

* * *

It was 7:15 when Hiro reached Unter den Linden. While Hiro had been down in the underground, it had started to rain outside. Cars drove past down the wide street, their wheels throwing up showers of water. Hiro buttoned up his jacket and set off for the Hotel Adlon. Beyond he could see the Brandenburg Gate. Now it was evening, the columns were lit with a strange golden light; the whole place looked very foreign and frightening.

When he arrived at the entrance of the Hotel Adlon, Hiro was nervous. A doorman stood outside the big revolving door. He was just moving forward with an umbrella to welcome someone arriving in a large silver Mercedes. The woman who climbed out of the back of the Mercedes was beautiful and dressed in very expensive clothes. Hiro stood to the side as she walked past him and into the hotel. As the revolving door turned around and around he could see bright lights and a shiny floor inside the hotel. It was so grand – Hiro had never been in a hotel like it before. He took a deep breath and went through the revolving door himself.

Over to one side there were several beautiful brown leather sofas and armchairs. A well-dressed young man was working at a laptop in one of the armchairs. On a sofa an older couple in evening clothes were chatting.

Hiro went over to the reception desk. The receptionist, a smartly-dressed young man with glasses, looked very surprised when he saw Hiro. He spoke to him in German.

Hiro cleared his throat. 'Do you speak English, please?'

The receptionist looked very doubtful about Hiro. Hiro knew what the man must think of him. Hiro was a poorly-dressed student standing at the desk of a five-star hotel. 'Of course,' the receptionist answered in perfect English. 'How may I help you?'

Hiro tried to speak in a strong voice. 'I'd like to see the manager, please.'

The receptionist gave a small nod. 'The manager is expecting you, of course ...?'

'No,' Hiro said.

The receptionist smiled weakly. 'Then I'm afraid I must ask you to arrange a meeting by telephone or email. I'm sure the manager will be very happy to see you then.'

Hiro tried to keep calm. His heart was beating hard. 'It's extremely important,' he said. 'I really must see the manager now.'

The receptionist smiled again and pressed a button at the side of the desk.

Hiro felt the bright lights burning down on his head. He was hot and exhausted. 'Please listen to me,' he said hopelessly. 'This really is an emergency!'

The receptionist continued to smile. Out of the corner of his eye, Hiro saw a man in uniform coming over.

'You must listen to me,' Hiro said, almost crying. 'There's going to be a murder here this evening! Please, you must believe me! Someone is planning to kill one of your guests!'

Chapter 13
Last hope!

Five minutes later Hiro was sitting at a table in a small office at the back of the hotel. The man in uniform was standing at the door. His arms were crossed and he looked angry. Hiro felt almost like a prisoner in a cell. He supposed the man at the door imagined he might try to run out of the room. Perhaps he thought he would behave badly and embarrass the guests. Hiro guessed that was the only reason he was not out on the street.

After a couple of minutes, another man appeared in the doorway. He was very smartly dressed, like the receptionist, and also wore glasses, but his hair was going grey at the sides. With a nod, he came round the table and sat opposite Hiro.

'Good evening,' he said. He didn't offer to shake hands. 'My name is Herr Fischer. I'm the duty manager here tonight. Could you tell me your name, please?'

'Adachi,' Hiro answered, politely dropping his head. 'Hiro Adachi.'

'From Japan?' the duty manager asked.

'Yes, I'm a student on a Study Year Abroad programme in England,' Hiro went on. 'I'm here in Berlin on holiday.'

'Excellent.' Fischer put his hands together very calmly on the table. 'Now, please could you explain what you told the receptionist? I understand you told him ...' The man paused. 'You told him something unpleasant would happen in the hotel tonight.'

Hiro knew he had to remain calm. If he seemed in any way crazy now, everything would be lost. 'Yes,' Hiro said. 'I'd better tell you immediately. I went to the police this morning, but they didn't believe me. But what I told them is completely true. Honestly!'

'I see ...' Fischer gave another patient nod.

'You see I discovered someone is planning a murder here in Room 319 this evening – it could be any time after eight o'clock. That's why it's an emergency.'

'Yes, I completely understand. But perhaps you'd better start from the beginning?' Fischer gave a weak smile.

Hiro nodded. 'Of course.' He began his story. He tried to tell it slowly and calmly, but from time to time it became impossible. When he described how the Shark had tried to kill him, then how Meier had kidnapped him and taken him to the 'safe house', it was really too horrible. But eventually Hiro came to the end, and looked up at Fischer helplessly. This man was his last hope!

Fischer watched Hiro for a moment or two, then nodded. 'Well, that's quite a story, Mr Adachi, quite a story indeed. Right, let's see if we can sort this out.' He paused and looked at Hiro seriously. 'What was the name of the old man on the train?

'Erik Björnson, I think,' Hiro said.

'Very good.' Fischer gave another nod. Immediately he reached across to the phone and pressed one of the buttons. A quick conversation in German followed. Hiro understood nothing except the name Erik Björnson. At last the conversation came to an end. Fischer put down the phone, then calmly put his hands together as before.

'Well, good news, Mr Adachi. First of all, I'm happy to tell you that there's no one by the name of Erik Björnson staying in the hotel – not in Room 319, nor in any other. And the guest in Room 319 is someone called Schmidt. Mr Schmidt is a regular customer, I'm told. Does this information make you feel any less worried?'

Hiro remained silent. Being Japanese, he always

felt it was polite to agree. But this time he simply couldn't do it. He moved uncomfortably in his seat.

'You still don't look happy, Mr Adachi,' Fischer continued.

Hiro didn't know what to say. He searched for words. 'But the Shark may be using another name,' he said at last. 'He may not even be staying at the hotel. Don't you see, he could walk in at any time?' Hiro began to feel helpless again. Surely Fischer could understand what he was saying? Why did everyone think he was just a crazy student from Japan?

Fischer looked at Hiro a little impatiently. 'I'm sorry, Mr Adachi, but I think we've done as much as possible. For anything further, I really think you must return to the police.'

'But in half an hour it'll be eight o'clock!' Hiro cried.

'Then perhaps you shouldn't waste any more time discussing it with me,' Fischer replied sharply.

Hiro didn't know what to do. His last chance was running away like sand through his fingers.

'I must ask you to leave now, Mr Adachi. We've done all we can,' Fischer said. He got to his feet. 'I'd like to thank you for your trouble. My colleague will show you out of the hotel. Hans!' Fischer said a few words in German to the man in uniform at the door.

Hiro had forgotten the man was there.

Hiro knew it was useless to say any more.

The man in uniform moved forward. 'Please follow me,' he said.

Hiro didn't argue. He followed the man through the corridors with his head down. He felt terribly tired.

They came out into the reception area. The bright lights hurt Hiro's eyes. The man led the way across towards the revolving door. Hiro's mind was completely empty; he had given all he could.

The man stopped at the door. '*Sayonara*,' he said in Japanese, with an unpleasant smile.

Hiro gave a shake of his head, but was too tired to say goodbye himself. He looked up at the door. It was already turning: an old man was just coming in, pulling a small case on wheels behind him. From his hat and clothes Hiro guessed the man must be a priest. Hiro stepped into the doorway and began moving through. At that moment the priest's eyes met Hiro's. They stared at him for one second only, then looked away, but there was something about the stare that Hiro recognised.

The next moment, as he stood on the pavement outside, Hiro realised who had just entered the hotel. It was the Shark.

Chapter 14
Inside the Hotel Adlon

For a second or two Hiro was completely unable to move. Even though the old man looked quite different dressed as a priest, Hiro was absolutely certain who it was. But the idea that the Shark might change his appearance had never really entered Hiro's head before. The memory of the priest he'd seen at the Brandenburg Gate came back to him – of course, that was the Shark!

He was sure too that the Shark had recognised him. Hiro's legs were shaking, but he couldn't stop staring in through the hotel window. The Shark was at the reception desk and was talking to the receptionist. The two of them seemed to be looking back at the door. Hiro turned away and walked quickly up the road.

What should he do? His first thought was to turn and go back into the hotel, but he stopped himself immediately. As well as being a stupid and dangerous thing to do, Hiro knew he wouldn't get past the door.

One of the men in uniform was sure to stop him at the entrance. Hiro knew as well that there was no point going back to the police – even if they listened to him, it would be too late. With a sick feeling in his stomach, he realised that if he were going to do anything, he would have to do it by himself.

Hiro walked up and down the street. 'Think!' he kept saying to himself. 'Come on! You must think!' The sick feeling got worse with every second that passed. The Shark was in the hotel. Hiro had to act fast!

He reached the end of the building, then stopped. A crazy idea came to him then.

There was no time to lose. Guessing that the hotel must have an underground car park, Hiro hurried back past the hotel entrance, then turned down the next side road. Thirty metres later, he found what he was looking for. A metal bar stretched across the entrance of the car park and there was an office to one side. Hiro walked past a couple of times, looking in at the office. A man was sitting at the window, with three or four TV screens above him, but he was more interested in the newspaper open on his desk.

After making sure there was no one watching, Hiro hurried beneath the office window, then round the metal bar. It was simple. He was in!

On one side of the car park he saw a row of expensive cars; on the other a sign read '*Ablieferungen*'. Hiro had no idea what it meant, but a few moments later a large white van with pictures of fruit and vegetables on the side arrived. Hiro guessed he must be near the hotel kitchens and that the sign he had seen meant 'Deliveries'.

There were voices just up ahead. Hiro dropped down behind a car and looked carefully round the next corner. A couple of young men were standing outside a doorway, smoking. They were wearing the white jackets of kitchen workers and they looked a little guilty, as if they were breaking some kind of rule. Hiro just waited and watched.

After five minutes, still laughing and chatting, they went back inside. Hiro waited half a minute longer, then ran up to the doorway where the two men had disappeared. The door was still half open. He pushed his way inside and found himself in a narrow corridor.

Up ahead he could hear the sounds of the kitchen. He moved forward. Halfway down the corridor there was a door on the left. He stopped and listened. No sound. Very carefully he opened the door and looked inside.

On one wall there was just a long shelf with huge cans of food, but when he looked on the other side of the room, he couldn't believe his luck. On the back of another door, Hiro saw three or four white jackets, similar to the ones the smokers had been wearing. If he put on one of these, Hiro thought, he might be able to get through the kitchens without being stopped.

There was no time for further thought. Hiro tried on the first jacket. It was far too big. He put it back and took the next. This time it was fine. He quickly buttoned the jacket all the way up to the neck and headed straight to the door.

Then he stopped. Perhaps it would be better if he was carrying something; it was less likely that he'd be stopped. Turning back, he picked up two of the big cans of food, then decided to take a third can too, as it would hide half of his face. Then he went out through the door.

He walked quickly. He couldn't stop and look around. He had to appear to know where he was going. He had to just trust his luck.

To his amazement, it went like a dream. Hiro walked straight down the corridor and a couple of seconds later found himself inside a huge kitchen.

There were three men over to the right standing near the ovens, but they didn't even look up, each busy at his job.

Hiro walked straight ahead, then reached a half-open door. As he did so, he heard someone coming in the other direction. Immediately, Hiro turned round and pushed his way through the door with his back – because he was carrying something it was the most natural thing to do. The other man hurried past without saying a word.

Once he was through the door, Hiro found himself in a hall. There were further doors to the right and left. Long corridors led away almost out of view. In front of him there were stairs and the doors of a lift.

Hiro thought about the lift. If it was a service lift, used only by hotel workers, it might go all the way to the top of the building. He took a deep breath and pressed the button. The lift doors opened immediately. He stepped inside, then came out again. The cans he'd been carrying had been useful, but now he needed something else.

Hiro put the cans down under the staircase, then noticed a pile of dirty sheets there. If he was carrying sheets, Hiro hoped he would again be mistaken for one of the hotel workers. He picked the sheets up and entered the lift just as the doors closed. He looked round for the buttons. Yes, it was just as he'd guessed! There were two floors below ground level, and seven above. If only his luck could continue. Surely, it was logical for Room 319 to be on the third floor!

He pressed the button showing '3'. The lift began to travel up.

Chapter 15
A little bit of Schubert

When the lift came to a stop, Hiro stepped out to find himself in a small area used only by hotel workers. Opposite the lift, there was a door. Hiro pushed it open. The next moment, as if going through a secret entrance hidden in the wall, he came out into a public corridor of the hotel. He was halfway along. The corridor, its floor covered in deep red carpet, stretched in both directions.

Hiro didn't know which way to go. He chose one way, but saw that the numbers on the doors were going up: 325, 327, 329. So he turned round, and the numbers on the doors began to go down, even numbers on the left, odd numbers on the right. He followed them down: 325, 323, 321. As he passed this last room, he felt his heart begin to beat very fast.

All of a sudden he was there: Room 319. He was about to knock, when he stopped himself. He realised he had no idea what he was going to say or do. His confidence suddenly left him. Was he really so certain a murder was about to take place?

Hiro didn't hear the door to the room behind him open. Out of nowhere, he heard a voice speaking in German.

Hiro turned to see a man of about thirty standing in the doorway of Room 320. The man looked quite tough – like a soldier perhaps, but in ordinary clothes.

Hiro felt helpless. 'I'm sorry, I don't understand German,' he said in English.

The man looked confused. 'You don't speak German?'

'No,' Hiro said.

The man narrowed his eyes. 'But you work here?'

Hiro felt weak at the knees. He'd forgotten the white jacket and the sheets he was carrying; now he couldn't think how to explain them. 'No, I'm a student,' he said quietly. 'But I must see the man in this room, Mr Schmidt. I have some important information for him.'

Immediately the man's body became tight. 'I think you'd better tell me first. I'm a colleague of Mr Schmidt.'

Hiro didn't know what to say.

'Well, I'm waiting,' the man went on.

Hiro wasn't sure if he could trust the man. But there was no time to decide. Hiro had to give an explanation. 'I came to see Mr Schmidt because ...' he began, then stopped. 'Well, his life might be in danger.'

Now the man's eyes became very sharp. 'We'd better talk about this in my room,' he said after a moment. His voice made it clear that Hiro shouldn't argue.

The man stood back and let Hiro go past into the room. As soon as they were both inside, the man shut the door quickly and looked through the eyehole to the corridor outside.

'Please sit down,' the man said, turning back to Hiro.

Hiro dropped the sheets behind the door and chose the nearest chair.

The man continued immediately. 'OK, you say you're a student?' He didn't sit down or wait for an answer. 'So, what information do you have for Mr Schmidt?'

'I was on the train to Berlin,' Hiro began, his voice shaking. 'By accident I looked at another man's phone and read a message – two messages, in fact. They talked about an assignment here in this hotel in

Room 319 this evening.'

The man looked surprised. 'Go on,' he said quickly.

'Well, the man on the train. He tried to kill me. And he's in the hotel now. I saw him only twenty minutes ago.'

At that, the man pulled up another chair and sat very close. His voice became very serious. 'This isn't a student joke, is it?' he said. 'It's very important. Do you understand?'

'Yes, I do.' Hiro looked straight back into the man's eyes. 'I was kidnapped as well,' he added after a moment. 'I've been very frightened.'

The man paused, then nodded. 'Do you know who Mr Schmidt really is?'

Hiro shook his head. 'No. What do you mean? Isn't Schmidt his real name?'

'No, it isn't.' The man watched Hiro closely. After a moment's thought, he went on: 'Listen, I'm going to tell you things which perhaps I shouldn't. But it seems there's very little time, so I'll have to take a chance. It doesn't matter who Schmidt is – it's enough to know he's someone extremely important. And for reasons I can't explain, Mr Schmidt is here in the hotel secretly.'

'OK,' Hiro answered.

'Well, I'm his bodyguard – his personal bodyguard – I'm here to make sure he's safe. Normally he has several bodyguards with him, but as he's here in secret I'm the only one with him tonight. Understand?'

Hiro nodded.

The man was very serious now, sitting forward closely. 'Now who is this man who's come to kill him? What does he look like?'

Hiro coughed. For a second he couldn't speak. 'He's old ... but there's something really frightening about him. He's like a shark – he's got the same eyes and teeth. On the train he said his name was Erik Björnson and that he was a businessman, but he came into the hotel this evening dressed as a priest.'

'A priest!' the man repeated.

'Yes, I'm sure of it,' replied Hiro.

The man jumped up from his chair and went to the door. For a moment he looked through the eyehole. Then he stood back. He thought for a second or two, then spoke again. 'OK, listen. There's no time to call my colleagues, so I'm going to need your help. What's your phone number?'

Hiro felt very frightened now, but he also had the wonderful feeling that he wasn't on his own any more

– someone had believed him at last. He told the man his number and the man typed it into his own phone. Immediately, he pressed 'Call'. Hiro's phone began to ring, then stopped.

'Right,' the man said, 'you've got my number now as well.' He paused and sat down opposite Hiro again. 'OK, this is what I want you to do. I'm going to try and get the pr—, I mean, Mr Schmidt, out of this place, or at least into another room. I want you to stay here. Stand by the door and look out through the eyehole. If this guy shows up – the priest, that is – the second you see him, call my number. Is that clear?'

'Yes,' Hiro answered.

'Good.' The man sat up. He looked at Hiro for a second, then said, 'What's your name?'

'Hiro Adachi.'

'Mine's Schubert, Franz Schubert,' the man replied. He immediately held up his hand. 'Yes, I know, there's a famous composer with the same name. My parents were crazy about classical music. Anyway, please call me Franz.'

'OK, Franz,' Hiro said.

'Great,' Schubert answered. He put a hand on Hiro's shoulder. 'You've done brilliantly, Hiro. And you've been very brave.'

He didn't delay any longer. Giving Hiro a nod, he got to his feet, picked up a small bag by the wall and went to the door. 'OK, this is it,' he said. As he did so, he reached inside his jacket and pulled out a gun. There was something very cold-looking about the black metal. Then he dropped his arm down by his side. 'See you in fifteen minutes,' he said in a whisper.

The next moment the man had gone. Silence fell inside the room.

Hiro looked at the door. Fear suddenly filled him. He was on his own again.

Chapter 16
A visit from the priest

Hiro stood there staring at the door for five or six seconds, then suddenly remembered he had a job to do. Without wasting another moment, he looked through the eyehole.

The view was better than he expected. He could see a couple of metres down the corridor in addition to the door of Room 319 opposite. Schubert was there at that moment. Hiro could see him looking up and down the corridor, the gun still down at his side.

About ten seconds later, the door to Room 319 opened. A woman, blonde and very attractive, wearing a red nightdress, stood in the doorway. She and Schubert talked for a moment, then she stepped back with a worried look on her face. Schubert went inside with her and the door closed immediately.

A minute passed. Hiro kept his eye to the door, only checking that Schubert's number was shown under 'Last Call' on his phone.

When he looked back someone had come into view in the corridor outside. Hiro's heart beat faster. Could it be the Shark? Hiro looked more closely. No, it was a boy of sixteen or seventeen, wearing a smart hotel uniform. In his hand he was carrying a message on a metal plate. But could it be one of the Shark's friends? Hiro watched through the eyehole as the boy came directly to Hiro's door and knocked.

Hiro didn't know what to do. He didn't want to open the door, but perhaps it really was a hotel worker. Perhaps the message was important – something Schubert should know. Hiro saw the boy look down the corridor, then heard him knock again, harder.

This time Hiro decided he must answer. Very carefully, he opened the door. It was only half-open when there was a dull sound twice: *dumf! dumf!* one after another. At the same moment the boy seemed to throw himself on Hiro, his arms flying round him almost like a lover. Hiro was knocked back, crashed against the wall, and fell to the floor. The boy came down on top of him and lay there without moving. The plate he'd been holding banged loudly against the door.

Hiro tried to get to his feet. He was so confused that for three or four seconds he still didn't understand that the boy had been shot. Then someone else appeared in the doorway. It was the Shark. He was still dressed as a priest, but he was now holding a silenced gun at his side. Hiro tried to speak, but no sound would come from his mouth.

'Yes, my friend, it's me,' said the Shark, with a sickly smile. 'I apologise for my violent entry.' He kicked the legs of the young hotel worker out of the way and closed the door immediately. 'A most unlucky young man. I needed some way to make you open the door,' he went on, 'and unfortunately for this boy, I chose him.' Then, getting down so he was level with Hiro, he continued, 'Right, now listen, my Japanese friend. I have very little time. I saw you come into this room and now I need some information.'

Still fighting to get his breath, Hiro managed to pull himself free from the body on top of him. As he did so, Hiro saw his jeans were covered in blood. For a second he thought he was bleeding, then he realised the blood belonged to the hotel worker. A scream grew in Hiro's throat, but wouldn't come out.

The Shark had his face close to Hiro's. His teeth seemed very bright. 'In a short time I am going to kill you.'

Hiro was completely unable to speak.

The Shark nodded his head. 'Yes, be sure of this – I will kill you. But I can do it in two ways.' He came even closer. 'The first way is with a bullet in the middle of the head. Like this ...' He pressed the gun into the middle of Hiro's forehead and made a clicking sound with his tongue, then pulled it away. 'You will not feel a thing. Very clean, very quick – you will like it!' He paused. 'Or I can shoot you in the stomach. The pain is terrible, please believe me.' His eyes seemed to dance with pleasure as he considered this. 'Yes, very terrible. That is why you Japanese commit *hara-kiri* by tearing a knife through the stomach – because death is so slow and you suffer so much. Very brave people, you Japanese.'

Now the Shark sat back on his heels, and watched Hiro thoughtfully. 'So that is your choice, my friend. If you tell me what I wish to know, *pop*, *pop* in the head, all very fast. If you don't, you will die very slowly. So, which will you choose?'

All the time the Shark was speaking, Hiro was trying to think what he could do. Was there nothing? Was this really the end? All day long he had been putting himself in danger, but somehow it hadn't seemed real. It had felt almost like a computer game which he could turn off when he'd had enough. Now this was completely real. He wanted to complain that the rules hadn't been properly explained, but he knew it was useless. He thought of Akiko suddenly. Would he never see her again after all?

'So, which is it to be?' The Shark pressed the gun hard into Hiro's stomach and smiled.

Hiro didn't answer. Thinking of Akiko had suddenly given him an idea. His phone was still in his hand. Could he manage to call Schubert without looking at the keys? He knew his phone so well – where all the different keys were and what they all did. If he could just get his hand in his pocket so it was out of view. All he needed to do then was bring up Schubert's number and press the 'Call' key.

The Shark was waiting for his answer. 'Well?'

'What do you want to know?' Hiro said quickly.

The Shark seemed surprised. 'So, you choose the head! This is very good. Right, I need to know this.'

Hiro had managed to sit up against the wall, and already he had his hand with his phone in it in his pocket. He turned the phone around in his hand. Was it the correct way up? He had to feel for the keys, but without pressing too hard!

'The man who went into Room 319,' the Shark began. 'He is a bodyguard, yes?'

'Yes,' Hiro answered. He had the phone the correct way up. He was sure of it. OK, now to bring up Schubert's number he had to press the 'Back' key.

'And he is the only bodyguard, yes?'

'Yes,' Hiro replied. His fingers felt around the keypad. Top right. That was the one to press. He did so without delay.

'And why has the bodyguard gone into the room?'

Hiro paused. 'He's going to move Schmidt to another room, I think.'

The Shark gave a short laugh. 'Schmidt! Ha! That's very good. And has the bodyguard called for any help?'

Hiro didn't answer. He was trying to think about the phone. The 'Call' key – it was top left, wasn't it? Or was it? Suddenly he wasn't so certain.

'Come on!' The Shark's eyes were full of sudden anger. 'Answer me! Are there more men coming? Do they know my description?'

'No!' Hiro answered. 'I don't know. I don't think so.'

'You are lying! You told him I was dressed as a priest, didn't you?'

Just as he was about to answer, Hiro remembered: the 'Call' key wasn't at the top; it was the one below it.

'Well?' the Shark shouted.

'Maybe,' Hiro said quietly.

'Ah, the truth at last!' The Shark sat back for a moment, looking pleased. 'Anyway, it does not matter. I have what I need.' He sat forward again. 'My friend, the time has come. I am sorry that it is not possible to get to know you better – you seem a very brave young man. But ...' The Shark lifted his hands as if in apology.

Hiro felt a tight ball of fear rise in his throat again. His fingers moved over the keys on his phone again. Was this right? Did he have the correct key? There was no time to think about it any more. He pressed hard with his thumb.

The Shark raised the gun and pointed it at Hiro's head.

Hiro thought he might cry. He had to keep the Shark talking. How long would it be before Schubert replied? Schubert was Hiro's last hope.

'Wait!' Hiro called hopelessly. 'Please, please, I know you're going to kill me, but will you do one thing for me?'

The old man suddenly gave a grandfatherly look. 'A dying wish?' His eyes went small again. 'What is it?'

Hiro had to keep the Shark talking for just a few seconds more. He said the first thing that came into his head. 'It's my girlfriend, Akiko. We broke up just before I came to Berlin. Will you send her a message for me?'

'Ha!' The Shark gave a sudden laugh. 'How romantic! Now I am to bring two lovers together in death!'

Hiro was unable to breathe. Perhaps he'd got the keys all wrong. Maybe there wasn't any hope ...

'And what is the tearful message you wish me to send?' The Shark had his caring look again.

'Please tell her ...' Hiro started.

'Yes?' said the Shark.

'I want you to tell her ...' Hiro began again.

The Shark suddenly tired of the game. 'Bah! You are trying to waste time. You think I am stupid?'

'No!' cried Hiro. All of a sudden there was a tiny sound. It came from Hiro's pocket.

There was silence in the room for a second.

Then it came again. It was a voice. 'Hiro?' it said quietly. Then more loudly, 'Hiro, it's Franz!'

Chapter 17
A surprise visitor

'What is that?' the Shark asked sharply.

'I don't know,' Hiro lied. He could hear Schubert saying his name repeatedly.

'It is your phone!' the Shark said. His eyes were on fire. 'Give it to me!'

Very slowly, Hiro took the phone from his pocket.

Schubert's voice was clear all of a sudden. 'Hiro? Hiro? What's going on?' Hiro could hardly believe it. The plan had worked!

But now the Shark was boiling with anger. He shouted a word in a foreign language that Hiro didn't recognise, then went back to English. 'What have you done? You have called this man!' He was shaking the gun right in front of Hiro's eyes. The Shark's face suddenly became very hard.

This is it, Hiro thought. Now comes the shot. Schubert had stopped speaking now. Perhaps he was crossing the corridor at that moment; perhaps he would crash through the door any second. But it didn't matter what the bodyguard did now. Hiro knew it would be too late. Helplessly, he put his hand up in front of his face as if he imagined he could stop the bullets. He prepared himself for the shot.

But it didn't come. Instead, the Shark pulled the phone from Hiro's hand.

'Who is this?' the Shark said angrily into the phone.

Hiro couldn't hear what Schubert replied. The gun was still pointing at Hiro's head and it was very difficult to think.

'Right,' the Shark went on in a new quieter voice. 'Listen to me. I believe you know who you are talking to. As you must know, I have the Japanese boy with me. If you try anything stupid, I will shoot him immediately. Is that clear?'

Again Hiro supposed that Schubert replied, but he had no idea what Schubert said. The Shark interrupted.

'All right, shut up! Listen to me. I am going to leave this hotel with the boy and you will not do anything to stop me. I have already killed one of the hotel workers. Now, this is what I want. Are you listening carefully?' He got quickly to his feet, made his way over to the door, and looked through the eyehole. Next he went over to the window, and looked out into the night. All the time he kept the gun pointing at Hiro. Very soon he came back.

'In a couple of minutes' time, the boy and I are going to leave this room. We will go down to the back entrance of the hotel – I want you to have a taxi waiting there for us. I will tell the driver where to go, but you will not attempt to follow the taxi. If there is trouble at any point, the Japanese boy will die. Is that clear? I will give you three minutes to arrange this. Call me back when everything is ready.'

The Shark pressed the 'End Call' key and dropped the phone into his pocket. Then he looked across to Hiro. 'This does not mean you will live after all,' he said. 'If I could, I would kill you twice!'

Listening to the Shark, Hiro felt strangely dead already. He was so tired; the last twenty-four hours had been so hard. It seemed as if he was watching himself in a crazy film, watching helplessly as it showed the story of his life.

'Get up!' the Shark said, coming towards him with the gun again.

Hiro climbed slowly to his feet. He wondered what was coming next.

'Now, go over to the door and pull the boy out of the way,' the Shark ordered.

Hiro felt ill again. He moved across and reached down for the boy's arms. It didn't hit him till then that the boy was really dead. Other than his grandfather, this was the first time Hiro had seen a dead person. When he tried to lift the boy's shoulders they felt so heavy and so warm. Was there really no life? Only ten minutes before, the boy had been knocking cheerfully on the door. Hiro wanted to cry.

The Shark was watching him closely. 'First time?' he asked coldly. 'Have no fear. Dead people don't usually complain.' He gave his horrible toothy smile for a moment, then his face went hard again. 'Come on – don't waste time.'

Hiro pulled at the body in his arms. 'I'm sorry,' he said under his breath. At last the body moved. As Hiro pulled the boy across the carpet a long bright red line of blood was left behind. Hiro thought he would be sick.

A moment later Hiro's phone rang again in the Shark's pocket. Hiro saw the Shark reach into his clothes, then a number of things happened very suddenly. First of all there was a very bright light and a terrific explosion, then the room went completely dark. At the same time a cloud of smoke filled the room. Hiro heard shots: again the *dumf! dumf!* of a silenced gun – then a loud cry of 'Aaghh!' followed by the crashing of furniture. After that there was a strange silence, like the end of the world. For a moment or two Hiro wondered if he was dead.

Then the lights came on again.

It took a little while for the smoke in the room to clear. When it did, Hiro saw that the door to the room had gone. It lay on the floor, broken in pieces. Standing over it was Schubert. On the floor opposite him lay the Shark. The old man was still alive, but he was holding his stomach very tightly. Already blood had started to appear through the priest's clothes; no matter how hard he held his stomach, he couldn't seem to stop it.

'Sorry to come in without knocking,' Schubert said coolly.

The Shark's eyes were tight with pain. Very slowly, he turned his head and looked directly at Hiro. His face had gone as white as a sheet, but his teeth still shone in the bright light.

In a quiet voice he said, 'I wish I had chosen another seat on the train.'

Chapter 18
A note of thanks

At two o'clock the next afternoon Hiro was sitting with Schubert in the Funkturm Restaurant, halfway up the famous TV and radio tower in the Spandau area of Berlin. It was a beautiful day. The sun was shining and from up there, you could see far across the city – huge roads busy with traffic, parks, even lakes and forests far away outside the city. In the distance a jet was just climbing into the air from the airport; it seemed to stick in the sky without moving.

'This restaurant is famous for its seafood,' Schubert said, looking at the menu. 'Why don't we go for that?'

'It's very expensive,' Hiro answered, noticing the prices.

'Don't worry about that,' Schubert said quickly. 'Someone very rich is paying. Let's make the most of it!'

Without discussing it any more, Schubert gave the waiter their order. When the waiter had gone, Schubert turned to the window. 'There. Berlin's not so bad, is it?' he said, pointing at the view.

Hiro was about to answer when Schubert's mobile phone rang. Schubert listened quietly to a message for half a minute or so, then excused himself and went off to a quiet part of the restaurant in order to continue the conversation.

While Schubert was gone, Hiro thought back over what had happened that morning. They had spent most of the time in Schubert's head office. 'The *Bundesamt für Verfassungsschutz* – Home Security,' Schubert had said by way of explanation. There, Hiro had spent two hours in front of a computer screen looking at photos of known criminals. The only man Hiro could definitely recognise was the driver who had picked him up with Meier. Hiro was disappointed, but Schubert wasn't. Once they found this man, he said darkly, it would be simple to get Meier and anyone else.

After that Schubert had said it was time for lunch. Schubert had put a blue emergency light on the roof of his BMW and they'd raced through the streets of Berlin, laughing like a pair of silly children. The journey had made Hiro feel happier than he had been for weeks – and very important.

Now, sitting up there in the restaurant, drink in hand, Hiro found it hard to believe all the things that had happened. He felt so safe and relaxed now, looking out across the city. Had the Shark really tried to kill him? It seemed like a dream. Had it all really happened?

As if in answer to Hiro's thoughts, Schubert came back to the table and sat down. He looked at Hiro before speaking.

'He's dead,' he said.

Hiro was confused for a moment.

'Our friend, the Shark. He died an hour ago.'

'Oh,' Hiro said. It felt as if a cold hand had run down his back. 'I'm sorry,' he said.

'Don't be sorry,' Schubert replied quickly. 'The man was a professional assassin. He made his living from death. He nearly killed you too.'

'Yes, I know,' Hiro answered.

'Anyway, let's give him his real name. I've just been told he was actually a Norwegian by the name of Karl-Henrik Johansen. Interpol, the International Police, have apparently been looking for him for years. He was wanted for eleven murders – one of them the president of a certain country in South America.'

Hiro didn't know what to say. He kept remembering the last time he had seen the Shark, as the old man was being carried to the ambulance, his face white with pain.

'Of course, it was because he came from abroad that he needed to collect a gun from Meier at the Brandenburg Gate. It would be much too dangerous to try and bring a gun into the country.'

Hiro went silent. Every mention now of the gun reminded Hiro of the young hotel worker.

Schubert was watching Hiro carefully. 'What's wrong?' he asked quietly. 'Is it the boy?'

Hiro nodded. 'I keep remembering ...'

Schubert reached out an arm. 'Try not to think about that.' Very gently, he added, 'If it helps at all, I can tell you he didn't suffer – he was killed immediately – the shots went through his heart.'

Neither man spoke for a while.

Hiro tried to think about something else. When he felt calmer again he said, 'I'm surprised the Shark decided to continue with the assassination plan after what happened.'

'Yes, it was a bad mistake.' Schubert looked at Hiro. 'I think he didn't like losing to a kid ...' Schubert seemed embarrassed for a moment, then went on quickly, 'I'm sorry. I'm not suggesting you're a kid –

but I guess the Shark thought of you like that. You were brilliant, you know,' Schubert added. 'What you did was very, very special.'

Now it was Hiro's turn to be embarrassed. Fortunately, at that moment the waiter arrived, so Hiro didn't need to answer. A huge plate of seafood was placed in front of him – Hiro suddenly realised he was terrifically hungry.

'*Guten Appetit*,' Schubert said.

'*Itadakimasu*,' Hiro replied.

They both ate happily in silence for a short time. Then Schubert sat back and looked closely at Hiro.

'Hiro, I need to talk to you about Mr Schmidt,' he began. 'You've been so extraordinarily brave it's only fair you should know something about him. But I'm very sorry, I still can't tell you his real name. I will say this though: the person whose life you saved is very, very important.'

'He's in the government?' Hiro asked.

Schubert looked directly at Hiro. 'I can't say. But he's someone of the very highest importance.'

'And you can't tell me why the Shark was hired to kill him either, I suppose ...' Hiro said.

Schubert gave a weak smile. 'Important people

make important enemies. We think Meier's men have been trying to kill Schmidt for months. After an earlier plan failed, it seems they decided to hire the best – that is, the Shark.'

Hiro was confused. 'Then why … why was Schmidt in a hotel with only you there – why was he there in secret?'

Schubert looked embarrassed again. After a moment he sat forward. 'Sometimes, Hiro, a man like Mr Schmidt has part of his life he wishes to keep private. That's why he meets his friend in a hotel. That's why I was the only bodyguard at the hotel. Do you understand what I'm saying?'

Hiro suddenly remembered the blonde woman who had opened the door of Schmidt's hotel room. 'You mean …' he said slowly.

'Somehow Meier and his men found out about Mr Schmidt's …' Schubert searched for the right word. 'Mr Schmidt's arrangement. When they did, they saw an opportunity to kill him.'

Hiro stared at Schubert. The man had told him as much as he could. Hiro nodded. 'I think I understand. Thank you for telling me.'

Schubert shook his head. 'No, no, we must thank

you.' He gave a little cough. 'Actually, while we're on that subject, I have something for you.' He reached into his pocket, pulled out an envelope and held it for a moment.

'Mr Schmidt asked me to give you this,' Schubert said and handed the envelope across.

Hiro looked at it for a moment or two.

'Go on, open it,' Schubert said.

Hiro did as he was told. Inside there was a second envelope and a small hand-written note. In English, the note read:

'Thank you so much for all you have done for me. You are a true *samurai*. Enjoy your trip.'

The note was signed with the single word: 'Schmidt'.

Hiro put down the note and opened the second envelope. Inside were ten completely new five-hundred-euro notes.

Chapter 19
A friendly word of advice

Two hours later, after a delicious lunch, Hiro and Schubert took the lift back down to the ground. They climbed into Schubert's BMW and set off back to the city centre. Schubert wasn't in any hurry and this time he drove much more slowly, window down, enjoying the sunshine.

After the excitement of the meal and the money from Schmidt, Hiro suddenly felt strangely empty. He had the odd feeling that he was returning to real life at last. In one way that was good: to know that he was safe was wonderful. But returning to reality also meant remembering his break-up with Akiko. How he wished he could share Schmidt's present with her!

It was as if Schubert could read his thoughts. The very next moment, looking across as he drove, Schubert asked, 'So, my friend, have you decided how to spend the money?'

Hiro bit his lip. He looked away, out of the window. 'I'm not sure,' he said quietly. 'I think I might save it.'

'What?' Schubert cried out. 'Come on! Don't be so boring. Enjoy part of it, at least. Fly somewhere! Go somewhere special! Take your girlfriend!'

It was the very worst thing Schubert could say. For a moment Hiro thought he might break into tears – the last twenty-four hours had taken all his strength. He bit his lip so hard this time, that he tasted blood.

Schubert noticed. 'Hey, did I say something wrong?' he asked more gently.

Hiro felt too tired to lie. 'I broke up with my girlfriend just before I came here,' he said at last.

Schubert looked embarrassed. 'I'm sorry.' Very quietly, he added, 'And it was her decision, not yours?'

Hiro nodded. 'I still don't know how it happened. I thought we were really happy together.' He closed his eyes as all the memories came back.

A hundred metres up the road Schubert stopped the car. 'Why don't you tell me about it?' he said. 'What happened?'

Hiro opened his eyes. They were next to a park. In the distance he could see a young couple walking hand-in-hand through the trees.

'I just don't understand,' Hiro began. He shook his head again. 'We had a terrible argument. We were planning a holiday together. Then, out of nowhere, this awful fight started.'

'Go on,' Schubert said.

'Well, this is going to sound crazy, but it was about my dog. I have a dog, Yuki – she's a golden retriever. Anyway, I have her photo on my phone as the screensaver. My girlfriend thought her photo should be there instead. I couldn't understand how she could be jealous of a dog.'

Schubert made an odd face. 'Really? It doesn't sound like a good reason to break up. Are you sure there wasn't something else?'

Hiro looked back at Schubert. 'What do you mean?'

'Well, people don't always talk about things directly, Hiro. Come on, you know that. Girls are the worst! There was probably another reason.'

Hiro tried to think back. He could remember the whole argument perfectly. He'd come to her room to talk, to tell her that he'd asked Daijiro and Ayumu and their girlfriends to join the trip. And Akiko had been fine with that. She'd said, 'Great, that's lovely.' She'd said, 'The more, the better!' She didn't seem to mind ... She didn't ...

Schubert broke into Hiro's thoughts. 'What is it?'

'I've just thought of something. When we were planning our trip, I thought it would be nice if we invited some others. You don't think ...?'

'Go on,' said Schubert.

'Well, it was a couple of guys and their girlfriends. You don't think she was jealous about that, do you?' Hiro asked. Just as he said it, a horrible idea came crashing into his head. Ayumu's girlfriend was Risa. Risa was from Hiro's college in Japan and he'd once invited her out. Perhaps Akiko had found out about that. Perhaps she thought ...

Schubert looked at Hiro and shook his head. 'Oh dear, my friend,' he said. 'You may be too clever for an international assassin, but it seems a young woman is too much for you. You were planning a romantic holiday for two, and then you invite another two girls along. I imagine the girls are pretty?'

Hiro felt suddenly very sick. 'So-so,' he answered, giving a small cough.

'Well, of course, she was jealous!' Schubert broke in. 'She simply pretended it was the dog, so she didn't have to admit it was the girls. What happened afterwards?'

'She said she never wanted to see me again,' Hiro replied.

'So, you believed her, I suppose. And being a brave *samurai*, you've been too proud to call her again. I guess you didn't apologise?' asked Schubert.

Hiro didn't say anything. He felt a mix of anger and sudden love for Schubert. The man had made him feel terribly stupid and small.

Schubert watched Hiro. For about ten seconds neither of them said anything. Then Schubert spoke again: 'Right, my friend, you've done something for me. Now I'm going to do something for you. Get out your phone.'

Hiro didn't argue.

'Now find me her number,' Schubert ordered.

Hiro's heart had begun to beat very hard. He selected 'Menu', then 'Phone book', then found Akiko's number.

'OK.' Schubert got out of the car. He walked round to the passenger door, opened it, then said very strongly, 'Right. Get out.' Hiro did as he was told.

Schubert pointed across the park. 'Do you see that seat over there? You're going to walk over to it and sit down. And then you're going to press that number.'

Hiro realised his lip was shaking. 'What shall I say?'

'You'll think of something,' Schubert replied.

Hiro didn't move for a moment or two. Then he felt Schubert's hand on his back, pushing him away.

Hiro walked slowly up the path. His legs felt heavy, almost too heavy to move. The sun was hot on the back of his neck as well and he felt a little sick from all the food. At last he reached the seat and sat down.

He looked across at the car. Schubert was sitting inside again, watching through the window. Hiro felt nearly as nervous as when the Shark had pointed the gun at his head. He looked at the phone and the photo of Akiko. Then he took a deep breath.

A couple of seconds later, he pressed 'Call'.

After reading

读后活动

Choose some of these activities.

1. Think of another title for *Berlin Express* and explain why it would be good.
2. If you were making a film of this story, which actor would you choose to play the Shark, and why?
3. Write an email to the author, Michael Austen, saying what you liked and didn't like about the story.
4. Write the phone conversation between Hiro and Akiko at the end of the story as a dialogue.
5. Write a paragraph as Hiro saying what you did with the 5,000 euros.
6. Choose one of the characters and write a one-paragraph personality description of him/her using what is in the book and your own ideas.
7. Choose one of the scenes involving two characters, and work with a partner to act it out with a dialogue.

8. Write an email from Hiro to his father telling him about his trip to Berlin – decide what to include and what to leave out.

9. Make a quiz about the story for other students, including some true/false questions and correct/incorrect sentences.

Learning guide | 学习指导

Chapter 1

New words 生词

- apparently /əˈpærəntli/ *ad.* 显然
- appear /əˈpɪə(r)/ *v.* 出现
- argument /ˈɑːgjumənt/ *n.* 争吵，争论
- bomb /bɒm/ *n.* 炸弹
- brave /breɪv/ *a.* 勇敢的
- chat /tʃæt/ *v.* 聊天儿
- choose /tʃuːz/ *v.* 选择
- confused /kənˈfjuːzd/ *a.* 困惑的
- conversation /ˌkɒnvəˈseɪʃn/ *n.* 对话
- crazy /ˈkreɪzi/ *a.* 疯狂的
- explode /ɪkˈspləʊd/ *v.* 爆炸
- immediately /ɪˈmiːdɪətli/ *ad.* 立即
- impossible /ɪmˈpɒsəbl/ *a.* 不可能的
- jealous /ˈdʒeləs/ *a.* 嫉妒的
- murder /ˈmɜːdə(r)/ *n.* 谋杀
- nod /nɒd/ *v.* 点头
- pause /pɔːz/ *v.* 停顿
- pretend /prɪˈtend/ *v.* 假装
- realise /ˈrɪəlaɪz/ *v.* 意识到
- reply /rɪˈplaɪ/ *v.* 回答，回复
- seem /siːm/ *v.* 似乎，好像

- sign /saɪn/ *n.* 标志
- thriller /ˈθrɪlə(r)/ *n.* 惊悚小说，惊悚片
- violent /ˈvaɪələnt/ *a.* 暴力的

Phrases & expressions 短语和表达

- all of a sudden 突然
- all the time 一直
- be about to 即将，刚要
- come out of nowhere 莫名其妙地出现（或发生）
- go on 继续
- look up 抬头看
- pick up 拿起
- race by 呼啸而过
- sit up 坐直
- take out 拿出
- turn on 打开

Cultural notes 文化点滴

- Eurostar: 欧洲之星，连接英国伦敦与法国巴黎、里尔，以及比利时布鲁塞尔的高速铁路系统。
- Shinkansen: 新干线，日本的高速铁路系统，以“子弹列车”闻名。

Reading exercises 阅读练习

1. True or false?

   a) Hiro was on a train.

   b) The train was in France.

   c) Hiro was studying German.

d) Hiro talked to a woman on the train.

e) Hiro had a dog called Yuki.

f) Hiro just broke up with Akiko.

g) The train was going slowly and Hiro was late.

2. How did Hiro feel when he thought about Akiko?
3. How did he feel at the end of the chapter?

Chapter 2

New words 生词

- area /ˈeəriə/ *n.* 区域
- attractive /əˈtræktɪv/ *a.* 迷人的
- book /bʊk/ *v.* 预订
- bottom /ˈbɒtəm/ *n.* 底部
- disappointed /dɪsəˈpɔɪntɪd/ *a.* 失望的
- equipment /ɪˈkwɪpmənt/ *n.* 装备
- nervous /ˈnɜːvəs/ *a.* 紧张的
- notice /ˈnəʊtɪs/ *v.* 注意到
- relax /rɪˈlæks/ *v.* 放松
- remind /rɪˈmaɪnd/ *v.* 使想起
- staircase /ˈsteəkeɪs/ *n.* 楼梯
- tiny /ˈtaɪni/ *a.* 微小的

Phrases & expressions 短语和表达

- a number of... 许多……
- after all 终究
- as if 好像

- for some reason 出于某种原因
- look away 转移目光
- of course 当然
- pull out 驶出
- remind sb. of... 使某人想起……
- take off 脱掉
- wait for... 等待……

Cultural notes 文化点滴

• Brandenburg Gate：勃兰登堡门，位于德国首都柏林的市中心，最初是柏林城墙的一道城门，因通往勃兰登堡而得名。现存的勃兰登堡门是一座希腊复古式建筑，由普鲁士国王腓特烈•威廉二世下令于1788年至1791年间建造，以纪念普鲁士在七年战争中取得的胜利。

• S-Bahn：城市快捷铁路，简称城市快铁。城市快铁不仅与U-Bahn（地铁）、Tram（有轨电车）、Bus（公共汽车）系统共同构成了城市内的公共交通系统，还类似通勤铁路系统，提供大都会区的中心城、近郊、远郊及卫星城之间，或是城市群中大小城镇间的快捷铁路运输。

• U-Bahn：城市内的地铁。

Reading exercises 阅读练习

1. Match the beginnings and the endings:

____1) Hiro changed trains

____2) The man who sat opposite Hiro

____3) The man was wearing grey clothes

____4) When the train braked suddenly,

_____5) The man's mobile phone

_____6) Hiro gave the man

a) a woman fell between Hiro and the man.

b) reminded him of a shark.

c) the wrong mobile phone back.

d) when he got to Köln.

e) and had very clean hands.

f) fell onto the seat next to Hiro.

2. What do you understand by the text message Hiro saw on the man's mobile phone?

Chapter 3

New words 生词

- act /ækt/ *v.* 行动
- apologise /əˈpɒlədʒaɪz/ *v.* 道歉
- beat /biːt/ *v.* 跳动
- colleague /ˈkɒliːg/ *n.* 同事
- discover /dɪˈskʌvə(r)/ *v.* 发现
- fill /fɪl/ *v.* 充满
- introduce /ɪntrəˈdjuːs/ *v.* 介绍
- private /ˈpraɪvət/ *a.* 私密的
- save /seɪv/ *v.* 保存
- shake /ʃeɪk/ *v.* 发抖
- silence /ˈsaɪləns/ *n.* 沉默
- silly/ˈsɪli/ *a.* 愚蠢的

Phrases & expressions 短语和表达

- in time 及时
- stare at... 凝视……

Reading exercises 阅读练习

1. Why did Hiro give the man the wrong phone?
2. What sort of book was Hiro reading and what effect did it have on him?
3. What did Hiro find out about the man from the earlier message?
4. What joke did the man make when he gave Hiro his phone back?
5. Who did the man tell Hiro he was?

Chapter 4

New words 生词

- certain /ˈsɜːtn/ *a.* 确定的
- direction /dəˈrekʃn/ *n.* 方向
- edge /edʒ/ *n.* 边缘
- frightening /ˈfraɪtnɪŋ/ *a.* 令人恐惧的
- information /ˌɪnfəˈmeɪʃn/ *n.* 信息
- persuade /pəˈsweɪd/ *v.* 劝说
- suppose /səˈpəuz/ *v.* 猜想

Phrases & expressions 短语和表达

- apologise to sb. 向某人道歉
- be close to... 靠近……

- even though 尽管
- get away from... 远离……，摆脱……
- get up 站起来
- in any case 无论如何
- look around 游览
- pull into... 进（站）
- sit forward 靠前坐
- think of... 考虑……
- turn around 转身
- walk across... 走过……

Reading exercise 阅读练习

Which of these statements is correct?

a) Hiro told the Shark something about his holiday plans.

b) The train was delayed for half an hour at Hannover.

c) In Berlin the Shark offered to help Hiro find his train.

d) The Shark leaded Hiro to the platform.

e) Hiro was very happy about this help because he didn't know German.

f) On the platform Hiro nearly fell under a train.

Chapter 5

New words 生词

- alive /əˈlaɪv/ *a.* 活着的
- awful /ˈɔːfl/ *a.* 可怕的
- ceiling /ˈsiːlɪŋ/ *n.* 天花板

- coffin /ˈkɒfɪn / *n.* 棺材
- disappear /dɪsəˈpɪə(r)/ *v.* 消失
- discuss /dɪˈskʌs/ *v.* 讨论
- escape /ɪˈskeɪp/ *n.* 逃跑工具（或方法）
- memory /ˈmeməri/ *n.* 记忆
- view /vjuː/ *n.* 视野

Phrases & expressions 短语和表达

- as long as 只要
- come back to sb. 使某人回忆起
- get off 下（车）
- seem like 似乎，好像
- teach sb. a lesson 给某人一个教训

Reading exercises 阅读练习

1. Who said or thought these things to or about whom?
   a) ‘You frightened me! You nearly fell!’
   b) ‘Why should an old man make me run off?’
   c) ‘You would like an egg?’
   d) ‘Leave Berlin alive – not in a coffin!’
   e) ‘Could you tell me where the nearest police station is?’
2. How did Hiro’s idea about what to do change in this chapter?

Chapter 6

New words 生词

- breath /breθ/ *n.* 呼吸

- camera /ˈkæmərə/ *n.* 相机
- cigarette /ˌsɪɡəˈret/ *n.* 香烟
- detective /dɪˈtektɪv / *n.* 侦探
- order /ˈɔːdə(r)/ *n.* 命令
- rubbish /ˈrʌbɪʃ/ *n.* 垃圾
- uniform /ˈjuːnɪfɔːm/ *n.* 制服

Phrases & expressions 短语和表达

- at any moment 随时
- break in 打断
- by accident 偶然
- come and go 来来往往
- in a mess 一团乱
- not...any more 不再……

Cultural note 文化点滴

• James Bond: 詹姆斯•邦德，《007》系列小说、电影的主角。小说原作者是英国作家、前特工伊恩•弗莱明。在故事里，詹姆斯•邦德是英国情报机构军情六处的特工，代号“007”，被授权可以干掉任何妨碍行动的人。

Reading exercises 阅读练习

1. Match the three police officers Hiro met with the descriptions.

____ 1) the first police officer

____ 2) Petra Müller

____ 3) the detective

a) was angry with Hiro

b) didn't understand much English

c) took a lot of notes

2. The detective suggested there were two reasons why Hiro thought the old man had tried to kill him. What were they?
3. How did Hiro feel at the end of his interview with the police?
4. What do you think Hiro would do now?

Chapter 7

New words 生词

- behaviour /bɪˈheɪvjə(r)/ *n.* 行为
- delete /dɪˈliːt/ *v.* 删除
- shine /ʃaɪn/ *v.* 照耀
- sightseeing /ˈsaɪtsiːɪŋ/ *n.* 观光
- stomach /ˈstʌmək/ *n.* 胃，腹部
- strength /streŋθ/ *n.* 力量

Phrases & expressions 短语和表达

- ask sb. for help 向某人求助
- at least 至少
- feel proud of... 因……感到自豪
- get in 进来
- have no idea 不知道
- knock over 撞倒
- ought to do sth. 应该做某事

Cultural notes 文化点滴

• Pariser Platz: 巴黎广场，德国首都柏林市中心的一个广场，位于勃兰登堡门内、菩提树下大街的西端。它得名于法国首都巴黎，以纪念 1814 年反法同盟取得巴黎战役的胜利，是柏林市最著名的地标之一。

• Unter den Linden: 菩提树下大街。它是柏林市中心重要的主干道，也是欧洲著名的林荫大道，长约 1.5 千米，宽 60 米。沿街有很多著名的建筑与地标，如德国历史博物馆、柏林洪堡大学、国家歌剧院、新岗哨等。

Reading exercise 阅读练习

Put Hiro's thoughts and actions in the order in which they occurred.

a) He got the U-bahn.
b) He rushed out of the hotel.
c) He remembered a humiliating story from the past.
d) He decided to go to the Brandenburg Gate.
e) He lay on his hotel bed for a long time.
f) He worried that he would be too late for the Shark's meeting.
g) He drank some green tea in a café.
h) He deleted all of Akiko's text messages from his phone.

Chapter 8

New words 生词

• grand /grænd/ *a.* 宏伟的

- recognise /ˈrekəgnaɪz/ *v.* 认出
- tourist /ˈtʊərɪst/ *n.* 游客

Phrases & expressions 短语和表达

- be full of... 充满……
- catch one's eye 吸引某人注意
- go off 离开
- if only 要是……多好
- look out for... 留心……
- out of sight 在视线之外
- plenty of... 大量……
- take a photo of... 给……拍照
- take place 发生

Reading exercises 阅读练习

1. Put the adjectives below into the correct sentences.

full	wide	important	dangerous	stupid

a) There was a ________ square in front of the Brandenburg Gate.
b) Hiro thought it was ________ to get too close to the Gate.
c) The square was ________ of tourists.
d) Hiro felt ________ when he didn't see the Shark at 13.00.
e) When the car stopped, the man said he had something ________ to say to Hiro.

2. Who do you think the man in the black BMW was, and what did he want?

Chapter 9

New words 生词

- department /dɪˈpɑːtmənt/ *n.* 部门
- furniture /ˈfɜːnɪtʃə(r)/ *n.* 家具
- leather /ˈleðə(r)/ *a.* 皮制的
- lounge /laʊndʒ/ *n.* 起居室
- pavement /ˈpeɪvmənt/ *n.* 人行道
- refuse /rɪˈfjuːz/ *v.* 拒绝
- shave /ʃeɪv/ *v.* 剃，刮
- smelly /ˈsmeli/ *a.* 有臭味的

Phrases & expressions 短语和表达

- make a decision 做决定
- pick sb. up 接某人
- point at... 指着……
- refuse to do sth. 拒绝做某事
- stand by... 站在……旁边
- talk to sb. 与某人谈话

Cultural note 文化点滴

- Bundesnachrichtendienst: 德国联邦情报局，成立于 1956 年，其主要任务是搜集和分析外国的军事、政治、技术和经济情报。

Reading exercises 阅读练习

1. Give short answers to these questions.
   a) What was the name of the man in the car?
   b) What was the BND?
   c) Where did they take Hiro?
   d) What was the flat like?
   e) Did Hiro believe what the man said?
   f) Who did he think the men were?
   g) Where did Hiro go?
   h) What did he decide to do?
2. What do you think would happen next?

Chapter 10

New words 生词

- expect /ɪkˈspekt/ *v.* 认为，料想
- trick /trɪk/ *n.* 骗局

Phrases & expressions 短语和表达

- be out of danger 脱离危险
- take a deep breath 深吸一口气

Reading exercises 阅读练习

1. True or false?
   a) Hiro got out of the flat and ran down the stairs.
   b) The men came out of the flat when he was on the next floor up.

c) Hiro made no noise because he wasn't wearing his shoes.

d) Hiro hid in a room in the roof of the building.

e) The driver went out onto the fire escape below Hiro.

f) The driver pretended to go back inside but stayed on the fire escape.

g) Hiro thought about his dog Yuki and asked her for help.

h) Hiro went down the fire escape and into the street.

i) He stopped a taxi and got into it.

j) He saw Meier coming out of the building.

2. What do you think Hiro would do next?

Chapter 11

New words 生词

- advertisement /əd'vɜːtɪsmənt/ *n.* 广告
- exhausted /ɪg'zɔːstɪd/ *a.* 疲惫的
- professional /prə'feʃənl/ *a.* 职业的
- snack /snæk/ *n.* 小吃

Phrases & expressions 短语和表达

- arrive at... 到达……
- get to one's feet 站起来
- go through 穿过，通过
- in fear of... 害怕……，担心……

Reading exercises 阅读练习

1. Choose the correct option.
   a) Did Hiro get off the bus in an old square or a modern one?
   b) Did Hiro sit with the people on the wall or on his own?
   c) Did Hiro go into a cinema or a theatre?
   d) Was Hiro hungry or thirsty?
   e) Was the film a western or a thriller?
   f) Did Hiro decide the Shark was a killer or not?
   g) Did Hiro think about what his father or his grandfather had said?
   h) Did Hiro fall asleep or watch the film?
2. Do you think Hiro would go back to his hotel? Why / Why not?

Chapter 12

New words 生词

- arrange /əˈreɪndʒ/ *v.* 安排
- manager /ˈmænɪdʒə(r)/ *n.* 经理
- receptionist /rɪˈsepʃənɪst/ *n.* 接待人员

Phrases & expressions 短语和表达

- be disappointed with sb. 对某人失望
- forget to do sth. 忘记做某事
- one after another 一个接一个
- set off 出发，启程

Cultural notes 文化点滴

- Alexanderplatz: 亚历山大广场。最早是羊毛和牲口的交易市场，20 世纪 60 年代改建成步行区。广场上最主要的建筑是广场酒店。位于广场的电视塔，高 368 米，是柏林最高的建筑。
- Mercedes: 梅赛德斯—奔驰，德国汽车品牌，被认为是世界上最成功的高档汽车品牌之一。
- Potsdamer Platz: 波茨坦广场。它是柏林的新中心，配套设施齐全，包括餐厅、购物长廊、剧场和电影院等，柏林的很多高楼都集中在这里，吸引着国内外游客。

Reading exercises 阅读练习

1. Match the beginnings and endings.

____ 1) When he left the cinema

____ 2) He decided to stay on the train

____ 3) A little later he felt bad

____ 4) Hiro felt very nervous

____ 5) Hiro asked the receptionist

____ 6) He tried to explain the situation

a) to kill some time before going back to his hotel.

b) when he entered the Hotel Adlon.

c) but he saw a man in uniform coming towards him.

d) Hiro thought he was going back to his hotel.

e) if he could talk to the hotel manager.

f) so he decided to do something.

2. Do you think they would let Hiro speak to the manager? Why / Why not?

Chapter 13

New words 生词

- horrible /ˈhɒrəbl/ *a.* 恐怖的
- prisoner /ˈprɪznə(r)/ *n.* 囚犯
- remain /rɪˈmeɪn/ *v.* 保持
- unpleasant /ʌnˈplez(ə)nt/ *a.* 使人不愉快的

Phrases & expressions 短语和表达

- as much as possible 尽可能多地
- first of all 首先
- from time to time 有时
- search for... 寻找……

Reading exercises 阅读练习

1. Who were these people?
   a) Herr Fischer
   b) Hans
   c) Mr Schmidt
   d) the old priest
2. What did Herr Fischer do about what Hiro told him?
3. How did Hiro recognise the Shark?

Chapter 14

New words 生词

- appearance /ə'pɪərəns/ *n.* 外表
- beneath /bɪ'ni:θ/ *prep.* 在……之下，往……下面
- trust /trʌst/ *v.* 信任，依赖

Phrases & expressions 短语和表达

- be interested in... 对……感兴趣
- be unable to do sth. 不能做某事
- even if 即使

Reading exercise 阅读练习

Put the things that Hiro did in the correct order.

a) He put on a jacket and carried three cans of food.
b) He pressed the button to call the service lift.
c) He went up in the lift.
d) He got into the service lift carrying the sheets.
e) He went into the underground car park.
f) He put the cans of food under the stairs.
g) He went through the kitchen.
h) He pressed the button for the third floor.
i) He waited for two kitchen workers to go inside.
j) He picked up a pile of dirty sheets.

Chapter 15

New words 生词

- carpet /ˈkɑːpɪt/ *n.* 地毯
- knee /niː/ *n.* 膝盖

Reading exercises 阅读练习

1. Which of these statements are correct?
   a) Hiro walked down the corridor to Room 319.
   b) Hiro knocked on the door of Room 319.
   c) A man came out of Room 320 and spoke to him in German.
   d) Hiro told the man he needed to speak to Mr Schmidt.
   e) The man took Hiro into Mr Schmidt's room.
   f) Hiro told the man about the Shark's plans and what had happened.
   g) The man was Mr Schmidt's bodyguard.
   h) The bodyguard told Hiro that the man in Room 319 was important.
   i) The bodyguard's name was Franz Schubert.
   j) The bodyguard gave Hiro a gun.
   k) The bodyguard told Hiro to go out into the corridor.
2. Who do you think Mr Schmidt really was? Why?
3. What do you think would happen next?

Chapter 16

New words 生词

- shoot /ʃuːt/ *v.* 射击，射中
- suffer /ˈsʌfə(r)/ *v.* 受痛苦
- unfortunately /ʌnˈfɔːtʃənətli/ *ad.* 不幸地

Phrases & expressions 短语和表达

- in addition to... 除……之外（还有）
- keep one's eye to... 留意……

Cultural note 文化点滴

- hara-kiri: 切腹自杀，日本武士所崇尚的一种死亡方式。

Reading exercises 阅读练习

1. Answer these questions.
   a) Who was in the corridor when Hiro first looked out of Room 320?
   b) Who opened the door of Room 319?
   c) Who came to Room 320 first?
   d) What happened to the boy?
   e) Who came to Room 320 immediately after?
2. What two options did the Shark give Hiro?
   a) Shoot him in the stomach or let him go free.
   b) Shoot him in the head or let him go free.
   c) Shoot him in the head or shoot him in the stomach.

3. What did Hiro do while he's giving the Shark the information?
4. How did Hiro make time for Schubert to answer his call?

Chapter 17

New words 生词

- interrupt /ˌɪntəˈrʌpt/ *v.* 打断
- repeatedly /rɪˈpiːtɪdli/ *ad.* 不停地

Phrases & expressions 短语和表达

- as white as a sheet 苍白如纸
- prepare for... 为……做准备
- pull at... 用力拉……

Reading exercises 阅读练习

1. Who said these things and to whom?
   a) 'What's going on?'
   b) 'You have called this man!'
   c) 'If you try anything stupid, I will shoot him immediately.'
   d) 'Dead people don't usually complain.'
   e) 'I'm sorry.'
   f) 'Sorry to come in without knocking.'
2. Why did the Shark say 'I wish I had chosen another seat on the train' to Hiro at the end of the chapter?

Chapter 18

New words 生词

- ambulance /ˈæmbjələns/ *n.* 救护车
- embarrassed /ɪmˈbærəst/ *a.* 尴尬的
- envelope /ˈenvələʊp/ *n.* 信封
- hire /ˈhaɪə(r)/ *v.* 雇用
- international /ˌɪntəˈnæʃnəl/ *a.* 国际的
- president /ˈprezɪdənt/ *n.* 总统

Phrases & expressions 短语和表达

- be famous for... 以……著名
- in the distance 在远处
- make one's living 谋生
- make the most of... 充分利用……

Cultural note 文化点滴

• Interpol: 国际刑警组织，成立于 1923 年，最初名为国际刑警委员会，总部设在奥地利首都维也纳。国际刑警组织保持政治中立，它并不会介入任何政治、军事、宗教或种族罪行，也不会介入非跨国罪案。

Reading exercise 阅读练习

Complete this summary.

This chapter took place in a very (1)________ restaurant where Hiro and Franz Schubert were having lunch. In the morning Hiro had looked at (2)________ of known criminals to try and pick out Meier and the driver. While they were eating, Schubert got a phone call to say that the Shark was (3)________ It seemed he was a Norwegian killer who was wanted by Interpol for eleven (4)________ Schubert told Hiro that he was extremely (5)________ to do what he had done alone and that Mr Schmidt had sent him something to (6)________ him. He gave Hiro an (7)________, and when Hiro opened it he found that there were five thousand (8)________ inside and a note from Mr Schmidt.

Chapter 19

New words 生词

- admit /ədˈmɪt/ *v.* 承认
- boring /ˈbɔːrɪŋ/ *a.* 无聊的
- reality /riˈæləti/ *n.* 现实
- sunshine /ˈsʌnʃaɪn/ *n.* 阳光

Phrases & expressions 短语和表达

- be jealous of... 吃……的醋；妒忌……
- break into tears 放声大哭
- break up with sb. 与某人分手
- share sth. with sb. 与某人分享某物

Reading exercises 阅读练习

1. How did Schubert help Hiro in this chapter?

2. What did Hiro realise about why Akiko had left him?
3. What did Schubert make Hiro do physically?
4. What do you think he said to Akiko?

Translation
参考译文

柏林快车

第 1 章　过去与未来

第5页

火车此刻正飞快地前进着。建筑物、田地和树木都飞一般一晃而过。一座桥从窗边闪过，接着是个车站。宏把脸凑近玻璃，想看清站名，但火车跑得太快，根本看不清。宏在想，这列火车是不是比世界闻名的日本新干线高速列车还要快。他抬头看了看车厢门上方的小屏幕，上面显示的速度是每小时 294 千米！他盯着数字慢慢增长。296……298……突然，速度达到了每小时 301 千米！啊，这说起来还挺令人兴奋的……

接着，他又想起那件事了。是的，但他又能跟谁说呢？如果是一个月前，甚至两周前，他会给秋子发短信。可自从他们分手以后，她再也不想收到他的消息了。“不要再给我发任何信息，因为我是不会回的，”她生气地告诉他说，“如果你宁愿在手机里放小雪的照片也不放我的，好啊，那就别再指望我做你的女朋友了！”

第6页

宏再一次伤心地望向窗外。他们这是到哪儿了？他知道他们已经离开了比利时，此时正在德国境内，因为在上一站之前他看到了一个标志，但接下来是哪个城市呢？是科隆吗？宏需要在科隆换乘。他在想是否应该问问坐在对面的中年女人，但就在他决定不问的时候，列车飞驰着驶过了一个村庄，而那个女人突然用英语和他说话了。

“哈！”她说，“那儿就是我住的村子！我还有一个小时就到家了。我们村儿到科隆只要十分钟！”

宏礼貌地笑了笑。那个女人看上去有点儿霸道，好像总是坐不住。

“但是你离家就远了……”她继续说，“你是日本人吗？”

宏点了点头。他不太想聊天儿，但显然那个女人想聊。“是的，”他说，“但是我在英国学习。我参加了一个‘国外学年’项目，现在放暑假了。”

“挺好！那你要去哪儿啊？”她继续问。

“柏林。我有欧铁通票。”宏回答说。接着看到她一脸困惑，宏猜自己最好解释一下，于是说道：“也就是我可以用这张票去欧洲的任何地方，柏林是我的第一站。”

第7页

“真令人兴奋！但是你是自己一个人旅行，真的很勇敢。”

宏停顿了一下。“我的朋友们……”他开始说，“我的朋友们……来不了了。”

“哦，那太糟糕了。”那个女人回应道。她正要说些别的，这时她的手机响了。她激动地在包里翻找手机，然后开始用德语对着手机大声讲话。

宏拿起自己的书。这是一本美国惊悚小说——他带着这本书练英语——内容相当刺激，他已经看了两起谋杀案了。但此时宏读不下去。他悲伤地思考着刚才跟那个女人说的话。他说的并不是事实。真实情况是他和秋子曾计划一起度假，但是争吵之后一切都变了。他们在一起时一直很开心。两人在英国上同一门课，他们在第一周就相遇了。他们之前也从来没有争吵过，后来竟然为了一条狗吃醋！真是疯了！

宏把手伸进口袋，拿出了自己的手机。他轻轻一动手机就打开了，他看着屏幕亮起，又看了一会儿屏保——打开手机时出现的那张图片。那是小雪的照片，小雪是一条 12 岁的金毛猎犬，长得很漂亮，是世界上最棒的狗。然后他从屏幕侧面的菜单里选择了“我的照片”。几乎立刻间，秋子的照片就出现了。这是秋子所有照片里他最喜欢的一张，是他带秋子去过生日时在餐馆拍的。她看上去那么高兴，那么漂亮！宏摇了摇头，很快返回到那张狗的照片。

第8页

那场争吵来得莫名其妙。他们一直在计划去西班牙南部的海滩度假。当他邀请他的朋友阿玉木和大次郎，以及他们的女朋友时，秋子看上去挺开心的。但是后来情况发生了变化。他说希望也能带小雪一起去，秋子突然就生气了。从此宏说的每一句话似乎都让秋子更加生气。她开始数落他的屏保，他知道的就是她喊着再也不想看见他了。这太难以置信了。前一秒他还有女朋友，下一秒就没有了。此时她显然是跟几个朋友去了苏格兰，可他甚至连这都无法确定。他们八个月的感情就像炸弹一样爆掉了。

突然，宏意识到一滴眼泪正从脸颊流过。他生气地擦掉眼泪。对面的女人还在大声地打电话，所以她没有看到宏流泪，但是这绝对不是一个 20 岁的日本小伙子应当有的举止。他急忙拿出欧洲火车线路图，假装在仔细研究。那天早晨他很早就离开了伦敦，乘坐欧洲之星列车前往比利时的布鲁塞尔。在那里他坐上了这趟开往科隆的列车，之后他将在科隆换乘前往柏林的列车。但是后面他要去哪儿呢？捷克共和国的首都布拉格，从柏林乘火车到那里仅需五个小时。然后，他可以去维也纳，或许吧。如果有时间，他甚至可以去布达佩斯。在这次旅行中他会游览多少个没去过的国家呢？如果那几个城市他都去了，那就是五个！

第9页

宏开始振作一些了。他坐直身子，又一次望向窗外飞驰而过的乡村。突然好像一切变得不同了，焕然一新。“对，”宏想，“我要度过一个令人兴奋而又惊险刺激的假期。我不要难过了。从这一刻起，秋子已经成为往事。不要再回首过去，从现在起，我只会向前看。”

第 2 章　遇见鲨鱼

第11页

列车继续飞驰了五分钟，然后开始减速。那个女人关上手机，忙着收拾自己的东西。

“到科隆了！”她愉快地说，然后站了起来，“现在我得去找我老公，你得去坐到柏林的车了，在第二站台。”

列车很快停了下来，宏跟着那个女人下车来到站台上。他们道别后，她立刻就朝一个正在楼梯底下等待的满面倦容的男人大喊起来。那个男人连忙朝她走过来，然后提着所有的包跟着她上了楼梯。

宏挤过人群来到第二站台。下一班火车要等半个小时。不知什么原因，他坐在火车站又一次感到孤单。火车一到站，他就上去了。他找到一个空座位坐下来，看着窗外的人群。宏注意到一个迷人的金发女孩儿拎着一个蓝色大提包上了火车。他心想这个女孩儿有没有可能会走过来坐在自己的对面，但她朝宏走了几步后，就挑了一个离他三排远的座位坐下了。宏有些失望。

第12页

接着，一个银灰色头发、身着灰色雨衣的男人上车了。他拖着一个带轮子的小行李箱。宏注视着他越走越近。他在车厢某处停了下来，跟那边的一个人说话。他笑的时候露出一排牙齿，宏不喜欢这个男人的长相。他的笑容、灰色的衣服和悄声行走的方式让宏想起了鲨鱼。这个男人朝他走来。宏希望他走过去，但是他没有。

“打扰一下，”这个男人露出同样的笑容用英文说，“这儿有人坐吗？”

宏别无选择。他旁边的座位和对面的两个座位都是空着的。“没人，”他说，“当然……”

“非常感谢。”这个男人回答。

他把行李箱推到座位底下，然后坐在了宏的对面。宏感到很不自在。这个男人的眼睛看起来很小，牙齿非常尖。宏再一次想到了鲨鱼。他想象着这个男人正笑着游向他。这微笑让宏感觉很冷，就像一只冰冷的手触到了他的脖颈。他看着这个男人脱下灰色的雨衣，然后从外套口袋里掏出手机，放在他们之间的桌子上。宏注意到了这个男人的手。这双手看起来极其干净，指甲修剪得整整齐齐。宏想这个人可能是个牙医。

第13页

火车驶出了车站。宏试图把视线从这个男人身上移开，继续看书，但是有什么东西让他不停地抬起头来看。此时男人已经从自己的箱子里拿出了一份报纸，戴上了眼镜。他看起来非常强壮，但从他那花白的头发看，宏猜想他有65岁左右了，甚至可能70岁了。过了一会儿，男人放下报纸，查看起手机来。他把手机拿在远处，看着屏幕。他的每一个动作都很仔细。他的手指在按键上轻轻移动着。过了几分钟，男人把手机放在桌子上，靠着座位闭上了眼睛。宏突然感觉心里平静了许多。这个男人让他很紧张，就像靠近了一只危险的动物。“对，”宏断定，“他不是人，他是一条鲨鱼。”

第14页

宏放松下来，开始读书。火车再次高速前进，而书里的内容也很刺激。宏再一次看表时已经过了四点钟。他看了看对面的男人。“很好，鲨鱼还在睡觉。”他想。

宏拿出他的旅行指南，想决定到达柏林后做些什么。他已经在克罗伊茨贝格区的一家价格便宜的阿尔玛宾馆预订了一个房间。但怎么到那里呢？好像是有一条叫“地铁”的地下铁路，还有一条地面的“城市快铁”。他应该乘坐哪条呢？

突然，火车紧急制动，随即发生了很多事情。制动太猛，致使一个正在车里行走的女人倒在了宏和鲨鱼之间的桌子上。她倒下时，把鲨鱼的报纸和手机从桌子上碰到了宏旁边的座位上。与此同时，鲨鱼跳了起来，快速伸出手，但他并没有去扶那个女人，而是把手伸到桌子对面试图取回他的东西。宏很惊讶。鲨鱼没能够到他的东西，但瞬间，他又变得友善起来。他一边说着德语，一边抓住女人的胳膊把她扶了起来。一番交谈之后，女人离开了。

第15页

鲨鱼又坐了下来。他立马说道：“我的手机在你那里吧。”

一时间宏没明白，接着他低头看向自己旁边的座位，看到这个男人的手机就在自己的夹克上。宏有些惊讶，因为他记得他把自己的手机放在那儿了。他拿起手机递了过去。

“对不起。”他说。

“没关系。”鲨鱼说着接过了手机。接手机时，他们的手碰到了一起。鲨鱼的手冰凉。“这些火车真是危险，”他继续说，“开得太快了！在这个国家旅行我总会紧张。”

“是的。”宏回答。

“能麻烦你一会儿吗？”男人说，“请帮我看一下座位。”

没等宏回答，他就拿起手机朝厕所走去。宏看着鲨鱼关上厕所门，接着看到门上方的灯亮了。

那会儿什么事情也没有发生，接着宏听到他的手机发出微弱的铃声，是收到短信的声音。他低头一看，在他的夹克下面发现了自己的手机。哦，手机还在。他的心微微一震，会是秋子发的吗？他拿起手机，按下按键打开短信。

第16页

有那么一两秒，他没太明白。他能看懂英语，却不理解短信的意思。他读了两遍。

“明天下午一点勃兰登堡门见。取装备和一半酬金。”

又过了两三秒，宏才意识到这不是他的手机。

第 3 章　有趣的错误

第17页

宏盯着手机。当然，他现在明白发生了什么——鲨鱼和他的手机一样都是诺基亚。他激动地查看信息时，没有注意到手机没有屏保，没有他的狗的照片。

好吧，这是一个小错误，没有什么好内疚的。鲨鱼从厕所回来时，宏就会把手机还给他并且道歉。这条信息看起来不是那么私密。

宏知道勃兰登堡门是柏林最著名的景点之一。那么，这个男人要在那儿跟人见面，要取走一些装备和一半酬金。这肯定不是什么隐私吧？

宏放下手机，抬头看了看。他想知道鲨鱼是否查看了他的手机，也发现了这个错误。厕所门上方的灯仍然亮着。或许就在此刻，鲨鱼正在读着秋子在分手前给宏发的情意绵绵的短信。宏保存了七八条这样的短信。

第18页

宏又读了一遍鲨鱼手机里的这条短信。可能是因为他读的那本书有很多凶杀情节，宏越看越觉得不舒服。这条信息好像有些奇怪，有些不太对劲儿。他停顿了片刻，然后做了件非常愚蠢的事情。他甚至在做之前就知道很愚蠢，但是实在太容易了。他按了鲨鱼手机上的“收件箱”按键，找到了信息列表。列表中的第一条信息，也就是他刚刚读过的那条，是一个叫“M”的人发来的。宏选择了下一条信息，也是“M”发来的。宏又抬起头看了看，很安全，厕所的灯还亮着。他打开了这条信息。手机的小屏幕上立刻出现了以下内容：

“柏林任务，阿德隆宾馆319房间，周二晚八点后。见面时付一半酬金，任务完成后付另一半。”

宏不确定自己看没看明白。他的心跳得很快。信息的一部分意思很明显：明天是周二，阿德隆宾馆一定在柏林。他也知道酬金的意思，就是办事的酬劳。但是其余的文字是什么意思？“任务”不是“工作”的另外一个说法吗？这个词听起来有点儿奇怪。“任务”这个词难道不是作家在惊悚小说里用来表达……？不，这想法太疯狂了！“一定是被我读的那本愚蠢的书影响的。”宏自言自语道。

第19页

下一刻他的心跳停止了。他抬头看时，厕所上面的灯已经灭了。不仅如此，门也开了，鲨鱼正从里面走出来。那个老头儿已经朝他往回走了。

宏不得不快速行动。他关掉信息，把手机放回旁边的座位。现在他可以放松了，鲨鱼永远不会知道宏看了他的信息。宏注视着这个男人走过来。

一秒后，宏意识到了自己的错误。鲨鱼当然会知道！上一条信息是他在厕所时收到的，宏当时就点开了。现在这条信息不会显示为“新信息”了，而是“已读”状态。就在鲨鱼回来时，宏拿起了手机。

鲨鱼还没坐下，就开始说话了。“哈，我的朋友！”他又露齿一笑，说道，“我刚刚经历了一件非常有趣的事情。在厕所时，我决定看看我的手机信息，但是当我打开手机的时候，我发现——”

第20页

“我拿着你的手机。”宏迅速说。

鲨鱼看了宏一会儿，接着似乎放松下来。宏有一种奇怪的感觉，他的话接得正是时候。

“是的，”他说，“我拿的是你的手机。这是你女朋友吗？”他短促地笑了一声，继续说：“她非常漂亮，叫什么名字？”鲨鱼越过桌子把宏的手机递过来。手机屏保显示着小雪的照片。

“小雪。”宏回答。

鲨鱼怪异地点点头。“是一条很漂亮的狗。我们用同款的诺基亚手机，真有意思！或许现在你可以把手机还给我了吗？”

手机已经拿在宏的手里。他递了过去，努力不让手颤抖。“我很抱歉，”他说，“来了一条信息，我打开了，才意识到……”

鲨鱼的眼睛眯了起来。他看了宏一会儿。“你当然会打开，这很正常。”他说完，看了看自己的手机。鲨鱼打开信息时，宏一动不动。宏看到他读完信息，又把手机关上了。“是的，一位生意伙伴发来的。”鲨鱼说。

第21页

他们沉默了一会儿，宏不知道说什么。接着鲨鱼慢慢点着头，笑了笑。“那么，既然我们知道了彼此的大秘密，我想咱们必须自我介绍一下了。我叫埃里克·比约恩森，来自瑞典，是商人。请问我有幸认识的这位是谁呢？”

第 4 章　援手

第22页

宏觉得有些热。火车好像开得更快了。

“我叫足立宏，”他说，“我来自日本。”

“是的，当然，”鲨鱼回应道，“日本是我最喜欢的国家之一。”他继续说。鲨鱼一边说一边往前坐了坐，微笑着伸出手。这笑容好像比之前更可怕了。

“很高兴见到您。”宏握着这个男人的手说。这只手又冷又潮湿，像鱼皮一样。

“非常荣幸，”鲨鱼回答，“那么，我猜你是个正在度假的学生？”

“是的，我正在环欧旅行。”宏回答。

“很好。柏林是你的第一站吗？”鲨鱼问。

“是的。”宏说。

“你要在柏林待几个晚上？柏林是个很令人兴奋的城市。”鲨鱼继续说。

“我不确定。”宏回答。

鲨鱼慢慢地点点头。“你肯定已经预订宾馆了吧？”

第23页

宏有种不安的感觉，鲨鱼问这些问题是有原因的。他突然不想告诉鲨鱼自己住在哪儿。“还没有，我打算四处转转。”他回答道。鲨鱼的眼睛眯了起来。

“可能住在克罗伊茨贝格。”宏快速补充道。他不知道这些信息够不够。

鲨鱼点点头。“或许我可以给你推荐个地方。摩德纳酒店呢？便宜，但是很舒适。”

“非常感谢，或许我会去试试。”宏回答说。

“我帮你打个电话。酒店老板是我的老朋友。”鲨鱼说着伸手去拿自己的手机。

宏不知如何是好。“谢谢，但是我打算在克罗伊茨贝格见一个人……一个日本朋友……和我来自同一个城市。”他怯怯地说。

两人都沉默了片刻。这是个谎言，宏能看出鲨鱼知道他在撒谎。宏感到非常燥热。

鲨鱼笑了。“当然，这只是一个想法。”他若有所思地看了宏一会儿，然后又说：“我必须向你道歉，我的朋友。我必须告诉你一件糟糕的事情。我是个非常愚蠢的老头儿，我看了你手机里的几条信息后，才意识到手机不是我的。我想你也是这样吧？”

第24页

宏感觉到一滴汗水顺着他的头发流了下来。火车上的灯突然显得十分明亮。“不是的，”他说，“只看了一条，关于你在勃兰登堡门会面的那条。”

又是长时间的沉默。宏想要擦去额头的汗水。沉默好像要永远持续下去。最后，男人又笑了笑，然后把目光转向别处。

* * *

火车在汉诺威延误了半个小时，所以他们到柏林时已经过了七点半。这是一个雨夜，天色已经暗了下来，因此城市里灯火通明。宏觉得放松多了。剩下的旅程里鲨鱼一直在睡觉——嗯，他的眼睛一直闭着。宏不确定他是否睡着了。此刻宏感觉自己很可笑，居然把这个老头儿想得那么坏。很明显，读了那本惊悚小说后，宏的想象力变得非常丰富。毕竟，这个男人年纪大得都可以当他的爷爷了，这样的人怎么可能会有危险呢？

他们终于进站了，火车站是座宏大的现代化建筑。宏拿起包站了起来。尽管他感觉好些了，却还是想尽快离开这个老头儿。

第25页

“认识您很高兴。”宏礼貌地说。

鲨鱼也站了起来。“你怎么去克罗伊茨贝格？”他问。

“我打算坐地铁。”宏说。

“不，不，那样不好。我给你指条最佳路线。”

宏的心怦怦直跳。“您真是太好了，但是我自己可以的。”

鲨鱼抓着宏的胳膊。“没事儿。”

宏感觉鲨鱼的手在拉着他往前走，拉下了火车。站台上人来人往，但是宏突然感到十分孤单。尽管他已说服自己，他的恐惧只是因为读了一本愚蠢的书，但宏还是意识到自己有一点儿发抖。他身处异国城市，语言不通，这个老头儿还让他感到害怕。

“跟着我，”鲨鱼说，“我会把你带到正确的城市快铁站台，然后把你留在那里。”

宏知道自己无法反驳。他努力保持冷静。“没事的，”他告诉自己，“五分钟以后我就又是自己一个人了。”

鲨鱼沿站台带路，一直走到一部下行的自动扶梯前。“你得坐城市快铁到弗里德里希大街，”他一边说一边与宏一起踏上运行的扶梯，“下一站就是，然后你要乘坐地铁到克罗伊茨贝格的哈勒门站。你明白了吗？”

第26页

鲨鱼的脸和宏的脸挨得很近。他的牙齿在车站的灯光下显得很亮。

“谢谢您，明白了。”宏回答道。

他们穿过了一个宽阔的大厅。一个大时钟下方，站着一家日本人。宏想向他们呼喊求救，但是没想出来说什么。片刻间他走过去了，无论如何都来不及了。

他们到了另外一部扶梯处，这次是上行。鲨鱼没有说话。宏告诉自己：“只要再过几分钟，我就安全了。”

他们来到另外一个站台。站台很宽，但是扶梯附近非常拥挤。

“过来，再往前走走空地儿就多一些。”鲨鱼说。

“我现在可以了，谢谢您。”宏说。

“不，我等会儿，”鲨鱼回答，“我必须确保你坐上对的车。”

他们走到站台三分之二的位置后停了下来。这里窄一些，因为这儿有一个很大的椅子。他们站得离站台边缘非常近。列车的声音使得宏转过身来。列车在快速驶入车站。他看到了车头的灯，司机正在往外看。宏感到鲨鱼向自己靠近了。

第27页

下一刻，宏突然想到了可能发生的事。站台上的每个人都在往前看，注视着列车。没有人向他们这边看。鲨鱼要推他，要把他推下站台，推到列车前面！

在最后一秒，宏从站台的边缘退了回来。与此同时，鲨鱼像是伸出了手，好像要掉下去似的。宏感到鲨鱼抓住了他的胳膊，但此时宏已经避开了危险。紧接着列车驶过去了，随后发出刺耳的制动声。几秒钟后列车停下了。

第 5 章　艰难的决定

第29页

“拜托！你吓到我了！你差点儿掉下去！”鲨鱼说。

宏惊恐地瞪大眼睛，说不出话来。老头儿的脸离宏的很近，他正紧紧地抓着宏的胳膊。

“你不能站得离站台边这么近！”鲨鱼继续说，“但这是你要坐的那班车，赶快上车吧！”他挪得离宏更近了。“一定要小心，年轻人。活着离开柏林——不要躺进棺材里！”

他们的目光相遇了一秒钟，然后宏感觉鲨鱼推了他一下。转眼间，宏发现自己已经在车上了，电动门在他身后关上了。

列车随即驶出了车站。宏没法儿动，他站在门口，看着外面站台上的鲨鱼。这个老头儿也没有动，他一直看着宏，直到列车开走。列车驶离了车站的灯火通明，鲨鱼从视线中消失了。

第30页

宏终于是一个人了。他想都没想就跌坐在座位上。突然他意识到自己浑身是汗。宏解开夹克。这是在做梦还是鲨鱼真的想杀了他？这似乎是个荒唐透顶的想法，但是宏想不出其他的解释。鲨鱼把他带到站台的边缘，挪到宏身后，然后伸手抓住他的胳膊。他最后说的什么？“活着离开柏林——不要躺进棺材里！”棺材不是他们用来装尸体的木箱子吗？宏忽然感到不寒而栗。他透过窗户凝视着这个城市，但什么也看不见，除了鲨鱼那双看向他的透着寒光的灰色眼睛。

宏永远不会知道那天晚上自己是怎么到宾馆的，那就像一场噩梦。过后回想起来，他记得自己在弗里德里希大街下了火车，然后跟着一群游客进了地铁。他完全不记得乘地铁时发生了什么，只记得听到报站“哈勒门！”，然后他按照旅行指南里的地图在黑暗中穿过了街道。不过他还记得那位个子矮小的老头儿艾伯特先生，宏按门铃的时候是他开的阿尔玛宾馆的门。艾伯特先生带着宏乘坐一部老式电梯到了三层，电梯大门是金属的，里面是木门。那天晚上这家宾馆对宏来说就像是第二个家，艾伯特先生就像是他的第二个父亲。宏倒在床上，几秒钟后就睡着了。

第31页

* * *

宏第二天早上醒来时，立刻回想起了一切。这个可怕的梦似乎无处可逃。他一睁开眼睛，就感觉鲨鱼像是正站在他的床边低声说：“活着离开柏林——不要躺进棺材里！”

宏的第一个想法是赶最早的火车离开这个城市。他可以直接去布拉格，或者可以去华沙或阿姆斯特丹——只要能离开柏林，任何地方都可以。

但是，当宏躺在床上仰望着天花板，想着站台上发生的一幕时，他愤怒起来。“凭什么一个老头儿就能让我跑掉？”他想。宏开始想当时为什么他会这么害怕。也许是在宾馆房间里安全了，宏想还是应该给鲨鱼一个教训，要让鲨鱼看看谁才是老大！

第32页

宏感到困惑，但是他躺得越久，就越生气。如果鲨鱼真的想把他推下站台，那么就是……宏坐了起来，热血沸腾。这个自称是埃里克·比约恩森的男人是谁？如果他真的想杀宏，一定是因为宏看了他手机里的信息。宏脑海中有一个挥之不去的想法——鲨鱼是个杀手。短信的意思就是他计划在那天晚上杀人。宏必须做点儿什么，但是做什么呢？

他想起了秋子。她总是知道要做什么。有那么一刻，他想给她打电话，但又停住了。不行，秋子说不想收到他的信息时，他回答说：“不要担心，你不会收到的！”他不愿意当那个示弱的人。如果她决定给他打电话，好吧，那另当别论。宏从床上跳起来，很气自己甚至考虑了一会儿这个想法。

宏去吃早饭的时候，艾伯特先生朝他友好地挥了挥手，把他带到桌子边。有一张桌子坐着一对年轻的美国夫妇，他们在讨论去万湖泛舟游玩。宏吃了一些麦片，想到如果能这样简单地待在这个城市该有多好。突然，他意识到艾伯特先生正站在他的肩旁。

第33页

“您想要个鸡蛋吗？”艾伯特先生轻声问道。

“抱歉，”宏回答，“不，不要鸡蛋，谢谢您。”接着，他脱口而出问道："您能告诉我最近的警察局在哪里吗？"

第 6 章　去警察局报案

第34页

半个小时后，宏来到了哈勒门的警察局外。抬头仰望这栋建筑，宏感觉刚刚燃起的信心突然不见了。这是一个巨大的灰色建筑，没有几扇窗户。站在那里，宏开始感到紧张。他想起了自己跟艾伯特先生撒的谎——他的相机被偷了，想报案。他多希望那是真的，他多希望自己从来没有遇到过鲨鱼，多希望自己担心的只是一部丢失的相机。忽然间他觉得来警察局似乎是一个巨大的错误，他甚至不再确定鲨鱼试图要杀他。

从一开始事情就不顺利，跟他说话的第一个警察不太懂英语，于是立刻去叫别人。宏在拥挤的等候室里紧张地等了半个小时，看着人来人往。

最后，一个身穿鲜艳的绿白相间制服的女警察出现了。她做了自我介绍，说自己叫佩特拉 · 穆勒，然后带着宏去了警察局里面的一间玻璃墙小办公室。

第35页

宏一开始讲得很糟糕。"我认为有一个老头儿要杀我。"他说。听到这里，警察挑了一下眉毛。"我看到了他手机里的几条信息，我想他今天晚上打算在阿德隆宾馆杀人，"宏继续说，"后来他企图在列车前面把我推下站台。"宏的话一股脑儿地往外冒，还不到半分钟，他就语无伦次了。

"好，"警察平静地说，"或许我们应该慢慢来。"宏不得不重复了一遍，讲述的同时警察记了几页笔录。最后她站起来，告诉宏她要叫别人来。

半个小时后，她再次出现了，这次带来了一个年纪大一些的男人。他很胖，身上有很浓的烟味儿。他没有穿制服，但宏断定他一定是个侦探。这位侦探没做自我介绍。他坐在桌子上，手臂交叉着。

“那么，你就是那个觉得有个老头儿要谋杀你的日本男孩儿，是这样吗？”侦探开口道。

宏不知道怎么回答。

第36页

“是这样吗？”侦探重复道。

“是的，没错。”宏最后说。

“你为什么认为这个老头儿想要杀你呢？”侦探问。

宏越来越紧张。“我跟您的同事解释过——”

“我不想知道你跟我同事解释了什么，我要你告诉我！”侦探生气地说。宏抬头看着侦探。他的情绪似乎非常糟糕——好像随时都会喊起来。

“我偶然看了这个老头儿手机里的几条信息，”宏低声说，“我们在火车上，我错拿了他的手机。”

“对，对，这些我都知道，”侦探不耐烦地说，“我想知道的是你为什么认为一个老头儿会因此想要杀你！”

宏又一次闻到了侦探呼出的烟味儿。“我觉得我在老头儿手机里看到的信息非常重要，”宏小声说，“有一条信息说他在阿德隆宾馆有个任务。”

侦探的眼睛一亮。“啊，一个任务！”他朝那个女警察笑了笑。“对不起，继续。”

宏觉得燥热。“另外一条信息说今天他将取走一半酬金和一些装备，在——”

第37页

“装备，嗯！”侦探打断他说，“你认为那是什么意思？”

“我不确定，”宏紧张地说，“我认为……”宏停住了。

“什么？”侦探说。

“我不确定，”宏回答说，“我认为那可能是一把枪。”他最后低下头说。

房间里一片寂静。宏能感觉到侦探的眼睛在盯着自己。最后，这个男人从桌旁站起来，开始在房间里走动。“好吧，我们暂时先不管这些。嗯，你说他想杀你，他到底是怎么做的？”

“我们在中心车站的站台上，”宏解释说，“他站在我身后，我觉得他要推我。”

“你觉得他要推你。”侦探缓缓地说。

“是的，他抓着我的胳膊。”宏继续说。

“他抓着你的胳膊。”侦探在他说完后重复道。

房间里一片寂静。宏感觉自己的脸涨得通红。大声说出自己的想法后，这事儿突然看上去很蠢。宏看到侦探正注视着自己。这个男人只是厌倦地点了点头，然后他说话了。

第38页

“我猜你喜欢看间谍片儿，是吗？詹姆斯·邦德、贾森·伯恩，这种垃圾片儿？”

宏没有抬头。

“我猜你知道，浪费警察的时间是一件很严重的事情。”侦探继续说。

“是的，我知道。”宏回答。

“你可以想象我们有多忙。”侦探说。

宏点点头。又是一阵寂静。

侦探最后继续说：“你一个人来柏林做什么？”

“我正在环欧旅行。”宏回答。

“我知道，但是为什么自己一个人？你的朋友呢？”侦探问。

“我……我本来打算跟女朋友一起度假，但是……我们俩刚分手。”宏轻声说。

“啊！所以我们现在明白了，失恋心碎了！”侦探摇着头朝门口走去。“听着，我的朋友，”他说，“没有人要杀你，今天晚上在阿德隆宾馆也不会发生任何谋杀案。你活在梦里呢，你看到一件事情，就想象出另外一件。这全是你的幻觉。现在，回宾馆去，装好行李，尽快乘火车回英国吧。给你女朋友买些花，这是我给你的建议。”

第39页

说完，他急匆匆地走出门，并在离开房间时对女警察用德语吩咐了几句。

宏低头看着地面。他以前从未感觉自己如此渺小。

第 7 章　痛苦的思考

第40页

宏返回宾馆，回到自己的房间，躺在床上，久久没有动弹。

他觉得很糟，警察不相信他。更糟糕的是，他们让他感觉自己又成了一个小男生，一个满脑子都是间谍故事，还为失去女朋友而哭鼻子的小男生。

这次去警察局让他想起了大约13岁时发生的事情，那并不是一段开心的回忆。一个大雪天，在去学校的路上，宏看到一个男人打碎了一辆汽车的侧窗，这个人爬进车里把车开走了。宏迅速写下车牌号，然后拨打了110紧急报警电话。整整一天宏都对自己的行为感到十分自豪，并且告诉了学校里的所有朋友。但是那天晚上宏的爸爸接到了警察局的电话，那个"偷"车的男人就是车主，车锁冻住了，而他又有急事需要用车。宏觉得自己很蠢，他从未把这个故事的结局告诉任何一个朋友。

第41页

现在他有了相同的感觉。侦探是怎么说的来着？他看到一件事就想象出另外一件。宏不会把自己那天早晨去警察局的事告诉任何人，他再也不会向警察寻求帮助了。

这样思考了半个小时后，宏突然从床上跳起来。像刚才那样躺在那里回顾过去，为自己感到难过，是软弱的，那是小男生的行为——就像把秋子发的所有情意绵绵的短信保存在手机里一样。他立刻拿起手机，找到秋子发的短信，准备删掉。他的手抖了一两秒钟。"删除所有信息？"的提示出现在屏幕上，他痛苦地叫了一声，按下了"确认"键。

随后，宏穿上夹克，匆匆走出了房间，差点儿撞倒了正在打扫走廊的艾伯特先生。他乘老式木电梯下去，很快来到了街上。他不知道自己要去哪里，也不知道要去做什么，但是现在阳光明媚，他想告诉自己他开心点儿了。

宏沿路走了一小段，在一家小咖啡馆停了下来，要了一杯绿茶。他端起茶杯，走到窗边坐下。望着窗外，看着路过的人们，他的思路开始变得清晰。他试图决定要做什么。既然是在度假，宏想自己真的应该去游览观光。于是他拿出旅行指南，开始阅读。

第42页

在旅行指南的第一页，他看到的第一个地方就是勃兰登堡门。宏盯着图片，这些文字好像从纸上跳到了他面前："勃兰登堡门是柏林最著名的景点，位于巴黎广场，在那儿也可以看到著名的阿德隆宾馆。"勃兰登堡门……阿德隆宾馆。宏又读了一遍，然后看了看手表，现在是十二点。一个小时后，鲨鱼就要跟人见面，他会取走枪，并收到一半酬金。

宏的胃有点儿难受，他的心开始狂跳，他闭上了眼睛。睁开眼睛时，他知道自己必须做什么了。他有勇气删除秋子的短信，那么现在他必须再勇敢一次。如果警察不愿意去勃兰登堡门，他只能自己去，一点之前赶到那里时间勉强够。

他立刻推开茶杯，匆忙穿过咖啡馆。他几乎是把一张五欧元的纸币扔到了柜台上，没有等着找零。一刻也不能浪费。

第43页

就在街角处他找到了一个地铁站，并在入口的地图前停了下来。坐哪一条线呢？他需要坐到菩提树下大街——那是离勃兰登堡门最近的地铁站。路线看起来非常复杂：他必须先去弗里德里希大街，然后换乘另一条地铁线。他想起旅行指南里说的，于是匆匆走进一家报刊亭买了一张地铁票，然后跑到站台上。

至少他不用等很长时间。很快列车到了，他跳了上去。他走过去靠着对面的门站着，紧张兴奋得坐不下来。

这段路好像没有尽头，尽管最多不超过五站地。到站后，他沿着站台跑，上楼梯下楼梯，来到另一条地铁线。

这一次等待的时间长一些。他刚刚错过了一班列车。现在已经十二点四十分了，离鲨鱼会面的时间只剩二十分钟了。宏在站台上踱来踱去。

十二点四十五分，列车终于来了。地铁一停下，宏就打开车门，跳上了车。现在只剩一站地了，最多需要三四分钟。他努力让自己冷静下来，做了几个深呼吸。列车驶出车站，钻进黑暗中疾驰。现在他一定能及时赶到吧？

第 8 章　短暂游览

第45页

五分钟后宏从地铁站出来时，发现自己来到了一条宽阔的街道上。沿街两边是整洁的商店和宾馆，几百米开外就是勃兰登堡门。宏看到了六根巨大的希腊风格的门柱，就像他在旅行指南里看到的一样，在其顶端，骏马和战车与天空交相辉映。

宏朝城门走着。十二点五十分了，现在他得格外小心。如果他想看到鲨鱼跟人会面的情景，就必须靠近城门，但是他还得确保自己不在他们的视线里，必须确保鲨鱼看不到他。

一开始没有问题，汽车沿街停了一路，宏紧挨着汽车走。在左手边他注意到了阿德隆宾馆的入口，那是一座带旋转门的宏伟建筑。如果宏的猜想正确，鲨鱼晚上就要在那里完成他的任务。

第46页

继续沿街前行变得越来越困难了。这条街通向一个宽阔的广场——巴黎广场。现在宏更容易被发现，但是这儿也有大量的汽车，很多车都很大，有深色的窗户。他走过这些车，越来越靠近城门，现在他能看出这门有多巨大了。很多人在柱子附近徘徊。他不知道应该做什么。鲨鱼或许会跟他朋友在门的另一侧会面，大部分游客都在那里，但是要靠近那里太危险了！现在是十二点五十五分了，要是他不这么容易被注意到就好了，要是他不是日本人就好了！

一辆长途客车停在了城门的另一侧，这引起了宏的注意。不一会儿，乘客们就从车门涌了出来。宏有了一个主意。这批游客都是欧洲人或美国人，但是如果他能绕到那边，一定很快就会出现一辆载满日本游客的长途客车。他开始往那边绕。

宏就要到了，这时就如他所料，一辆长途客车停在了路边。紧接着，三四十个各种年龄的日本游客急匆匆地下来了。宏走过去加入了他们的队伍。

第47页

听到自己国家的语言，宏想大声哭出来，但是他忍住了，他必须留意鲨鱼。旅游团里有几个人从保护套里拿出相机，急匆匆地往前走，宏跟着他们一起走。走近城门时，他的视线搜寻着柱子的下方，没看到鲨鱼。他看了看手表，正好一点钟。

宏研究了一下城门周围的人，有几个人在走来走去，要么抬头看柱子，要么站在那儿拍照，没有任何一个人看起来像鲨鱼。唯一一个超过五十岁的是一位神父，穿着黑色长袍，站在左边较远的地方。宏感到失望。他这么勇敢地战胜恐惧，难道要一无所获吗？宏注意到一个人去了神父旁边，他们两个人走到一根柱子后面，接着就从宏的视线中消失了。

五分钟过去了，宏开始思考他是不是犯了一个错误，他应该回到城门的另一侧吗？

一个拄着拐杖的老头儿缓缓走过，宏的心跳停了一下。他看不到这个男人的脸。这是假装需要拄拐杖的鲨鱼吗？宏走过去想要看清楚这个男人的脸，但是又停了下来。一个身材矮小的老太太，可能有八十岁了，走到了老头儿身边。

第48页

宏摇摇头，看看手表：一点十分。难道鲨鱼真的不来了吗？宏开始思考各种可能性。如果，手机拿错了以后，鲨鱼改了见面的时间或地点怎么办？

一只手搭在了宏的肩膀上，吓了他一跳。一瞬间他觉得肯定是鲨鱼，随后他苦笑了一下。一个从长途客车上下来的日本女人冲他微笑着，手里举着相机。她想让宏帮她和朋友在城门前合影，她说的是日语。宏觉得自己很蠢——他沉浸在这样的幻想中，连自己的母语也没听出来。他按要求给她们照了相，并把相机还给她们，然后看了看手表，现在是一点二十分。

那么，鲨鱼终究是不会来了。宏觉得自己很傻。“或许警察局的侦探是对的，”他想，“或许我应该乘第一班火车回英国。”他径直朝城门走去，不再躲在日本游客中间，然后往地铁站走去。现在他只想离开柏林，离开这个愚蠢的城市。

第49页

宏离地铁站不到五十米了，这时身后不远处一辆汽车的声音使得他回头看了看。一辆深色窗户的黑色宝马车停在他身边。与此同时，后面的车窗开了，一个深色头发的男人看向窗外。

“是足立宏先生吗？”这个男人用英语问，接着没有等宏回答就说，“我想跟你谈一谈，这非常重要。”

第 9 章　安全屋

第50页

宏看向车里。"什么事?"他说。他惊讶得说不出别的。

"我叫卡尔·迈耶。"那个男人接着说。他穿得非常得体。"我在联邦情报局工作。联邦情报局是德国警方的一个部门，负责国外的情报工作。我们需要跟你谈谈，请上车吧。"

与此同时，汽车司机下来了。他剃着光头，穿着一件黑色的皮夹克，看起来非常强悍。他为宏打开了车后门。

宏感觉心跳得很快。"嗯，当然可以。"他说。他非常紧张，不确定是否应该上车，但是司机将手放到了宏的肩膀上。宏上了车，坐在卡尔·迈耶旁边。紧接着，砰的一声，司机把后门关上，然后坐进了前排，把汽车开走了。这一切发生得如此之快，宏都来不及思考。

"不要担心，我的朋友，"迈耶说，"你跟我们在一起非常安全。"他伸出手说："很高兴认识你，足立先生，你是一位非常勇敢的年轻人。"

第51页

宏跟这个男人握了握手。汽车已经离开了菩提树下大街，快速穿过几条街道。宏从镜子里看到司机正看着他，司机的脸上有一道长长的疤痕。

"咱们要去哪儿?"宏问卡尔·迈耶。

"只是去一个我们能更安静地谈话的地方，足立先生。"那个男人脸上浮现出奇怪的笑容。从汽车的镜子里，宏看到司机也笑了。

宏开始感到不安。警察怎么知道他在哪里？他现在真希望自己没有上这辆车。为什么这俩人都没有出示警官证之类的东西？

汽车继续快速行驶着。没有人说话。宏不知道他们在哪儿。

最后宏终于问了出来。“你们是怎么知道在哪儿能找到我的？”他咳嗽了一声说。

迈耶没有看他。“我们跟踪你一段时间了。”他平静地说。

宏看到司机又笑了。

“你的意思是从我今天早晨去警察局开始？”宏问。

听到这里，迈耶扭头看了看，他注视了宏一两秒钟，然后轻轻点点头。“是的，是这样的，你说的一些事情我们想再核查一下。”

第52页

宏尽最大努力让自己放松下来。至少他现在能解释他们是怎么把他接走的了。

最后他们拐进一条小道，绕到一栋大楼后面，宏不确定这是办公室还是公寓。接着汽车驶过人行道，开进一个地下停车场，汽车明亮的前灯在黑暗中亮起。宏觉得有点儿难受。

他们停在一部电梯对面。司机立刻下了车，告诉宏跟着他走。宏从车里下来，片刻后，迈耶赶上了他们。

“这就是我们所说的‘安全屋’，”迈耶说，“我们用它面谈，以及其他活动。自然，大多数人我们不能带去总部。请跟我来。”

迈耶带路来到电梯口，按了墙上一个按钮，门立刻开了。他们三个人进去了，里面又脏又臭，一个空啤酒罐倒在地上。迈耶厌烦地把它踢开了。

电梯慢慢上升，接着门开了。他们走出来时，面前有两扇棕色的门，一条长长的走廊通向右边，有上下楼梯。

第53页

司机从口袋里掏出一把钥匙，打开左边的门，迈耶带他们进去了。当宏看到这是一套简单的公寓时，他放松了一点儿。在门厅的一侧有卧室和洗手间，正前方是厨房，右边是客厅。他们走进客厅，迈耶打开了灯。家具非常少，只有一张沙发配两把扶手椅、一个茶几、一台电视机，但是好像没有人在这里住。墙上没有照片，房间里没有任何让人感觉很温暖的东西。迈耶坐在其中一把扶手椅上。

“请坐。”他指着沙发说。“或许你想来杯咖啡？”他补充道。

“不，谢谢。”宏回答。

迈耶快速用德语跟司机说了几句，司机离开去了厨房。宏不喜欢在这个房间的感觉，这儿又冷又奇怪。

迈耶似乎着急开始。“那么，你今天早晨去警察局时，那位普通警察，也就是——”

“我觉得他们不相信我。”宏打断他说。

第54页

迈耶的眼睛眯了起来。“是的，你说得对，他们是一帮蠢货。事实上我们偶然在电脑上看到了你的笔录，便立刻展开了行动。”

“我明白了。”宏回答，语气中带着一点儿不确定。

迈耶看起来不太自在。“好，现在用你自己的话告诉我你跟普通警察说了什么，这很重要。当然，你跟他们说了火车上那个老头儿的事儿，关于你在他手机里看到的信息，你告诉他们什么了？”迈耶此时往前坐了坐，仔细注视着宏。宏没有回答。一切都不对劲儿，他心想。这俩男人不对劲儿，房间不对劲儿，问题也不对劲儿。他不知道要做什么。

“说吧？”迈耶不耐烦地说。

宏看着这个男人。“对不起，请问有洗手间吗？”

迈耶一时间看起来很恼火，然后似乎放松下来。“有，当然有，”他笑着说，“我带你去。”

“谢谢。”宏回答。

迈耶带宏走出客厅，给他打开了洗手间的门。宏进去后关上了门。他听到迈耶离开去了厨房，开始跟司机说话。宏坐在浴缸边上，双手抱头，他必须想清楚。“这俩男人不是真正的警察，也不是国外情报人员，”他告诉自己，“他们一定是鲨鱼的朋友，或许他们是从勃兰登堡门开始跟踪我的。是的，肯定是这样的！或许鲨鱼早就已经在城门那儿了。他在那里跟这俩人见了面，他们看到我后就决定跟踪我，让我上他们的车。那么现在他们要把我怎么样呢？”

第55页

宏四处看了看。他必须逃跑。除了从门出去，洗手间里没有别的出口。他能做什么呢？

第56页

他站起来，走到门口去听外面的动静。他能听到迈耶在用德语说话，听起来他像是回到了客厅，可能正在打电话。

宏的大脑快速运转。他想：“他们是想确定我知道些什么。”这就是为什么是迈耶在问问题，而不是鲨鱼——通过伪装成警察，他们希望从宏那里得到更多信息。如果鲨鱼问这些问题，宏可能拒绝回答。但是他们一旦听到了一切，肯定会杀了他。“我后脑勺会挨一枪，”宏告诉自己，“或者，也可能是从窗户掉下去。”

没有时间去想了。宏又环顾了一下洗手间，随后做出了决定。他只有一次机会，如果想逃跑，就必须是现在。

他站在门旁边。

第 10 章 逃跑!

第57页

宏小心翼翼地打开洗手间的门，向门厅探出头去。他是对的，迈耶回到了客厅，正在低着头全神贯注地打电话。司机在厨房，宏看不见。

宏深吸了一口气，他仅有几秒钟时间到前门。他脱掉鞋子，悄悄地穿过门厅，仅仅走了五步，就来到了前门。如果门是锁着的，他就完蛋了……

他很幸运。随着微弱的声响，门开了。宏走出去，来到了主走廊，接着径直跑向楼梯。

仅仅往下跑了三四个台阶，他就意识到自己犯了一个错误。“不行，”他想，“一旦他们意识到我逃跑了，会以为我往下跑了，所以我必须往上跑。”他一步两个台阶转身往上跑，刚来到上面一层，就听到那俩男人喊着德语跑出了公寓。他听到他们在电梯外面停了下来。

第58页

宏只能猜他们在喊什么，但是接着就听到了他们匆匆下楼的脚步声。

那么，现在该干什么呢？宏的心快速跳动着。不一会儿他们就会意识到宏没有下去，就会飞奔上楼。防火梯！在这样的地方应该有一个防火梯，但是在哪儿呢？

他一口气往上跑了两层楼，鞋还拿在手里。然后他到了顶楼——没有楼梯了，只有另外一条走廊。他可以听到那俩男人在下面远处叫喊着，然后是一阵安静。他们在听他的动静，听他的脚步声。接着宏听到其中的一个人上来了。

这里什么也没有。宏沿着走廊的方向跑。走廊的尽头有扇门。他推了一下，门开了。

宏发现自己来到了外面的防火梯——大楼外侧通到楼下的金属楼梯。应该下去吗？他别无选择。那个跑上来的男人随时都会顺着走廊看过来，然后看到他。

宏往下走了几个台阶，随后听到下面某个地方的门开了。他跑回上面，看见那个司机出来上了防火梯，就在他下面两层楼的地方。宏看到他往下看了看，接着，就在那个男人要抬头的时候，宏缩回去紧紧地靠在墙上。他的心狂乱地跳着。那个男人当然能看到他！两三秒钟过去了，宏听到那个男人朝楼里面喊，接着回到了楼里，门砰的一声关上了。宏又深吸了一口气，他脱离危险了！

第59页

宏正准备下楼，这时又有什么东西让他停了下来，是楼下传来的轻微声响还是别的什么？他回想起以前看过的一部电影。这是一个骗局！那个司机的喊叫是一个骗局，目的是让宏认为这条路是安全的——那个男人大声地关上门，但是此刻他还在防火梯外面往上看着。宏没有动，他闭上眼睛，秋子的面容浮现在他的脑海。“请帮帮我。”他轻声说。漫长的十秒钟过去了，接下来从下面传来轻轻的呼唤。随后，门又关上了。这一次宏知道那个男人真的进去了。

宏下楼梯时，腿一直在颤抖。现在他没有停下来或者四处张望，脑袋里只想着下到一层。有一次他差点儿摔倒，但设法稳住了，三十秒后他来到了地面。

第60页

他发现自己在两栋大楼之间的小道上，路通向大楼前面的大街。他能看到行人走过，就是要走这条路。宏快速走向大街。他刚到那儿，就看到一辆巴士停在了大约十米外的路边。他没有犹豫，朝它跑去。司机正要关门的时候，他跑到了车边。宏几乎是冲了上去，跌坐在座位上。

巴士开走时，宏透过他刚刚逃离的那栋大楼的玻璃门看到了迈耶。宏低下头躲开迈耶的视线，假装系鞋带。又过了两三分钟，他才敢抬起头环顾四周。随后，他掏出手机，打开秋子的照片。“谢谢，”他低语道，“谢谢你。”然后，他小声说：“我非常抱歉删除了你的信息，这是一个严重的错误。”

第 11 章　暴风眼

第61页

十分钟后，巴士驶进一个巨大的现代广场停了下来。大部分乘客都匆匆下了车。宏此时不想自己一个人待在任何地方，于是跟着他们走，在人群之中他感觉更安全，这个地方很热闹，到处是购物的人。即便如此，他还是禁不住大约每隔十秒钟就回头看看。迈耶看到他坐上巴士了吗？猜到巴士要去哪儿了吗？

广场的一边有一面墙，很多人坐在那里。附近有个卖烤肉的商贩，坐在墙边的人大部分都在吃小吃，他们看起来轻松愉快，聊着天儿，互相拍照。宏走过去，坐在他们中间。作为一个日本人，他知道自己很容易被注意到，但是有这么多人在周围，一定不会有危险吧。

宏一坐下来，就意识到自己是多么疲惫。他的第一个想法就是回到宾馆倒在床上，没有烦恼地再睡一觉就太棒了。他感觉仿佛已经在担惊受怕中生活好几周了。自从遇到鲨鱼之后，真的只过了二十四小时吗？

第62页

在广场较远的那一边，一个电影院的标志吸引了宏的目光。突然间，在黑暗中安全地与世隔绝几个小时的想法似乎很棒，就像暴风雨中的宁静时刻。他们把它叫什么——暴风眼？他一刻也没耽搁，站起来急忙朝电影院入口走去。他一边走，一边禁不住回头看，但好像没有人在跟着他。

他到了售票处，发现自己很幸运，一部新的惊悚片正要开始放映。他付了钱，买了个热狗，进去找座位。

进去时，正在放广告，但好在里面很暗。他还是担心有人可能在跟踪，于是选择了一个后面的座位。他想，这样一来，就可以看到每一个进来的人了。他坐下来，立刻开始吃热狗。早餐以后，宏就一直没有想起吃东西，他吃惊地发现自己原来这么饿。

电影很快开始了，谢天谢地，是英语版，不是德语版。电影还是让宏感觉很累，每个人物都语速特别快，宏发现很难跟上。他开始思考那一天发生的事情，有些问题他必须找出答案。

第63页

宏现在十分确定鲨鱼是一名刺客——一个职业杀手。那个老头儿来柏林是要杀人。那条短信说，“柏林任务，阿德隆宾馆 319 房间，周二晚上八点以后”，所以谋杀行动会在那天晚上的阿德隆宾馆 319 房间实施。他推测鲨鱼还是去了勃兰登堡门，大概跟迈耶一起去的。他们在那里看到宏，决定让迈耶跟踪他。他们想知道警察是否知道了阿德隆宾馆的事情。如果知道，鲨鱼可能就不得不取消他的计划。是的，一定是这样！那么谋杀呢？还会继续吗？宏应该做什么呢？

宏思考着这些问题，忧虑着下一步的行动，感觉非常疲惫。对他来说，这次旅行似乎变成了某种考验。他记起祖父在弥留之际跟他说过的话。老人病得很厉害，不几天就要去世了，所以家人都来跟他告别。老人抓着宏的胳膊，把他拉到床边。“生活是一场考验，宏，”他说，“要让我骄傲。”此时这些话在宏的耳边响起。这就是老人的意思吗？宏精疲力尽地摇了摇头，闭上了眼睛，电影配乐就像海浪拍打沙滩一样冲击着他。

第64页

宏接下来知道的事情，就是一个穿白衬衫系黑领带的男人把胳膊搭在他的肩膀上。那个男人正使劲儿摇他。他先用德语说了些什么，然后试着用英语说：“嘿！不要在这里睡觉！”

宏摇了摇头。“什么？”他说。他不清楚自己在哪里，然后他想起来了。

“不要睡觉！”穿白衬衫的男人仍在摇他。“如果你想睡觉，去宾馆睡！”

宏直起身。“对不起。”

那个男人露出生气的表情，但是收拾了座位底下的垃圾后就离开了。

宏看了看手表：五点四十五分！他无法相信，电影剩余的部分他一定是一直在睡觉。

他站起来。接着，过去二十四小时的所有回忆让他猛然清醒：鲨鱼……勃兰登堡门……迈耶和安全屋……

宏又倒在座位上，双手捂着头。

第 12 章　耳边的回响

第65页

宏离开电影院时已经快六点了。天空乌云密布，广场四周的广告灯牌像在夜里一样亮晃晃。有一瞬间宏觉得自己可能回到了东京，这让他非常想家，但是他不在家里。电影院上方的一个牌子写着“亚历山大广场”。他看了看旅行指南里的地图，想弄清楚自己在哪儿。

亚历山大广场在地图上不难找。他看到这里离自己的宾馆不远，坐地铁只有七八站地。宏不假思索地朝地铁入口走去。他不是很清楚自己回到宾馆房间后要做什么，他想自己只是打算躺在床上看看书或者电视，直到睡着，然后第二天早上就离开柏林。他的旅行好像很失败，但他已经受够了。害怕、疲惫、寒冷，他不是已经竭尽全力了吗？他已经很勇敢了，不顾自身安危——祖父不会对他失望的。宏现在为什么不可以悄悄离开柏林去其他地方呢？

第66页

亚历山大广场站很大，人来人往。那儿好像有多条线，有地上的，也有地下的。他又查了一遍地图，选择了地铁二号线，得换乘一次。

没等多久列车就到了。他上车坐在角落，车厢很满。他打量着车厢里形形色色的人，男男女女、老老少少、富人穷人，有的显然是在下班回家的路上，有的则是刚开始夜生活。他注视着一对儿跟他年龄相仿的情侣，他们在一起亲密地交谈，并快速吻了一下。多么美好啊，他想。能够在这世上如此无忧无虑，该多好啊。车站一个接一个匆匆而过。宏出神地看着这个充满活力的城市在眼前掠过。

列车到达波茨坦广场，宏才意识到自己坐过站了。看着列车里面的地图，宏发现自己忘了早点儿下来换乘六号地铁。他摇了摇头，跳起来朝车门走去。

第67页

就在迈出车厢之前，他停了下来。“我为什么不继续这趟旅程呢？”他想，“我可以一直坐到这条线的终点，再坐回来，这样至少可以消磨一些时间。”

他笑着回到座位，邻座的女人看起来很惊讶。列车驶离了站台。宏看了看手表：六点三十五分。他努力让自己放松下来。

五分钟以后，他知道这不可能了，他如坐针毡。他不能就这么回到宾馆，假装对鲨鱼的计划一无所知，一个声音在他耳边低语。在宏决定回自己宾馆房间的那一刻，这个声音就开始了。“懦夫！”它在说，“你根本不勇敢，你就是一个懦夫！”

每经过一站，这种感觉就变得更糟。他又看了看手表，现在是六点四十五分了。这时他突然想起来，大约一小时后很可能会发生一起谋杀！宏开始感觉很难受。他是唯一知道鲨鱼计划的人，是唯一可能阻止他们的人。他必须回去，必须做点儿什么。当列车驶入下一站时，宏已经等在门口准备回去了。

* * *

第68页

宏到达菩提树下大街时已经七点十五分了。宏在地铁里时，外面就开始下雨了。车辆开过宽阔的街道，车轮溅起了水花。宏扣上夹克的扣子，向阿德隆宾馆出发。他能看到远处的勃兰登堡门。夜幕降临，几根门柱被有些奇怪的金色灯光照亮，整个地方看起来非常怪异恐怖。

宏到达阿德隆宾馆门口时，非常紧张。一个门童站在大旋转门外面，他正打着伞上前迎接一位乘坐大型银色梅赛德斯车到来的人。从梅赛德斯车后座出来的这个女人很漂亮，穿着非常昂贵的衣服。她经过宏走进宾馆时，宏站到了一边。随着旋转门一圈圈地旋转，他能看到宾馆里耀眼的灯饰和闪光的地面。这里是如此富丽堂皇——宏以前从没来过这样的宾馆。他深吸了口气，从旋转门走了进去。

在宾馆里面，一侧摆着几张漂亮的棕色皮沙发和扶手椅。一个穿着考究的年轻男人正坐在其中一张扶手椅上用笔记本工作，一对身穿晚礼服、年纪稍大的夫妇正在沙发上聊天儿。

第69页

宏走到前台，接待人员是一个衣着得体、戴着眼镜的小伙子。他见到宏时看上去很惊讶。他用德语跟宏说话。

宏清了清喉咙。“请问您能说英语吗？”

接待人员似乎对宏有些疑惑。宏知道那个小伙子是怎么看自己的。一个衣着寒酸的学生却站在五星级宾馆的前台。“当然，”接待人员用极好的英语回答，“有什么可以帮您？”

宏努力用强有力的声音说：“我想见经理，劳驾了。”

接待人员微微点了点头。“经理知道您要来访，肯定是这样的吧……？”

“不。”宏说。

接待人员勉强笑了笑。“那么恐怕我必须请您打电话或发邮件来安排会面。我确定经理那时会很高兴见您的。”

宏努力保持冷静。他的心在剧烈跳动。“这无比重要，”他说，

“我真的必须现在就见到经理。”

第70页

接待人员又笑了，摁下了桌子侧面的按钮。

宏感觉明亮的灯要把他的脑袋烤坏了，他又热又累。“请听我说，”他绝望地说，“这真的是紧急情况！”

接待人员继续笑着。从眼角的余光里，宏看到一个穿制服的男人走过来了。

“您必须听我说，”宏几乎喊起来，“今晚这里有人会被谋杀！拜托，您必须相信我！有人计划刺杀你们的一位客人！”

第 13 章　最后的希望！

第71页

五分钟以后，宏坐在了宾馆后面的一间小办公室的桌边。那个穿制服的男人站在门口，他的胳膊交叉着，看起来很生气。宏觉得自己像是牢房里的罪犯。他推测门口的男人觉得他可能会试图从房间里跑出去，或许他以为宏的举止会很恶劣，让宾客难堪。宏猜想那是他没被赶到大街上去的唯一原因。

几分钟后，另一个男人出现在门口。他衣着非常得体，就像那个接待人员一样，也戴着眼镜，但是他的双鬓已经花白。他点了一下头，绕过桌子，坐在宏对面。

“晚上好，”他说，他没有主动握手，“我是费希尔先生，是今天晚上这里的值班经理。能请您告诉我您的名字吗？”

“足立，”宏礼貌地低下头回答，“足立宏。”

“来自日本？”值班经理问。

第72页

“是的，我是学生，正在参加英国的一个‘国外学年’项目，”宏继续说，“我来柏林度假。”

“很好。”费希尔非常冷静地把双手叠放在桌子上。“现在，请您解释一下您跟接待人员说的话，可以吗？我知道您跟他说……”那个男人停顿了一下，“您跟他说今天晚上宾馆里会发生一些不愉快的事情。”

宏知道自己必须保持冷静。如果他现在有任何一点儿看上去疯狂的举动，那么一切都会白费。“是的，”宏说，“我最好立刻告诉您。我今天早晨去过警察局，但是他们不相信我，可我跟他们说的完全属实，是实话！”

“我明白了……”费希尔又耐心地点点头。

“您看，我发现有人计划今天晚上在319房间实施谋杀，可能在晚上八点以后的任何时间，所以这十分紧急。”

“是的，我完全理解，但是或许您最好从头说起？”费希尔勉强笑了笑。

宏点点头。“当然。”他开始讲述自己的故事。他尽量冷静地娓娓道来，但是有时却做不到。当他讲到鲨鱼如何企图杀他，接着迈耶如何绑架了他，并把他带到“安全屋”时，这真的是太恐怖了。但是最终宏说完了，他无助地抬头看着费希尔，这个男人是他最后的希望了！

第73页

费希尔看了宏一会儿，点点头。“嗯，真是个不寻常的故事，足立先生，真是不寻常的故事。好的，咱们看看能否解决这件事。”他停下来认真地看着宏。“火车上的那位老人叫什么名字？”

“埃里克·比约恩森，我觉得是。”宏说。

“很好。”费希尔再次点了点头。他立刻伸手去够电话，按了其中一个按钮，接下来是一段快速的德语对话。除了埃里克·比约恩森这个名字之外，宏一点儿都听不懂。最后对话结束了，费希尔放下电话，然后像刚才一样冷静地把手叠放在一起。

“嗯，好消息，足立先生。首先，我很高兴地告诉您，住在宾馆的客人里没有叫埃里克·比约恩森的——319房间里没有，其他房间也没有。319房间的客人叫施密特。我了解到施密特先生是一位常客。这些信息让您没那么担心了吧？”

宏沉默着。作为日本人，他一直觉得认同别人是礼貌的行为，但是这次他就是做不到。他在座位上不自在地动了动。

第74页

“您看起来仍然不开心，足立先生。”费希尔继续说。

宏不知道要说什么，他搜索着话语。“但是鲨鱼可能用别的名字，”他最后说，“他甚至可能没住在这家宾馆。您不明白吗，他可以随时走进来？”宏又开始感到无助。费希尔肯定能理解他说的吧？为什么每个人都认为他只是一个来自日本的疯学生？

费希尔有点儿不耐烦地看着宏。“抱歉，足立先生，但是我想我们已经尽力了。至于其他事情，我真的认为您应该去找警察。”

“但是还有半个小时就八点了！”宏喊着。

“那么或许您不应该再浪费更多时间跟我讨论了。”费希尔厉声回答。

宏不知如何是好。他最后的机会正像沙子一般从指缝中流走。

“现在我必须请您离开，足立先生。我们已经把能做的都做了。”费希尔说。他站了起来。“谢谢，您费心了。我同事会带您离开宾馆。汉斯!”费希尔用德语对门口穿制服的男人说了几句话。宏都忘了他在那里。

第75页

宏知道再多说什么也没用了。

那个穿制服的男人走上前。“请跟我来。”他说。

宏没有争辩。他低着头跟着那个男人穿过走廊。他感到极度疲惫。

他们来到了接待区。明亮的灯刺痛了宏的眼睛。那个男人带路朝对面的旋转门走去。宏的大脑一片空白，他已经尽了最大努力。

那个男人在门口停了下来。“再见。”他带着令人不舒服的微笑用日语说。

宏摇了摇头，他太累了，连再见也说不出。他抬头看着门，门已经在转动了，一个老头儿正好走进来，他拖着一个带轮子的小箱子。从他的帽子和衣服来看，宏猜测他肯定是个牧师。宏迈入旋转门，开始往外走，就在那时牧师与宏的视线相遇了。牧师仅盯了宏一秒钟，就把目光移开了，但是他的注视让宏觉得似曾相识。

下一刻，当宏站在外面的人行道上时，他意识到刚刚走进宾馆的那个人是谁了，就是鲨鱼。

第 14 章　进入阿德隆宾馆

第76页

有一两秒钟时间宏完全动不了。尽管那个老头儿打扮成牧师的样子，看起来很不一样，但是宏十分确定他是谁。然而宏真的从来没有想过鲨鱼可能会乔装打扮。宏回想起在勃兰登堡门看到的那个牧师——当然，那就是鲨鱼！

他也确信鲨鱼已经认出他来了。宏的腿在颤抖，但是他忍不住透过宾馆窗户往里看去。鲨鱼正在前台与接待人员说话。这两个人好像正回头朝门口看。宏转过身去，沿马路快步走着。

他应该做什么呢？他的第一个想法就是转身回宾馆去，但是他立刻打消了这个念头。这样做不但愚蠢又危险，而且宏知道他根本进不了大门。其中一个穿制服的男人肯定会在门口拦住他。宏还知道回警察局也没有意义了，即使他们听他的话，也太迟了。他的胃里一阵恶心，他意识到如果自己打算有什么行动，只能亲自去做。

第77页

宏在街上徘徊。“思考！”他一直对自己说，“快！你必须思考！”每过一秒钟，这种恶心的感觉就增加一分。鲨鱼在宾馆里，宏必须快速行动！

他走到大楼的尽头，随后停下了。这时一个疯狂的想法闪过脑海。

没有时间可浪费了。他猜想宾馆肯定有地下停车场，宏赶紧往回走，走过宾馆入口，然后拐到旁边的路上。走了 30 米后，他发现了自己要找的地方。一根金属栏杆横在停车场的入口，旁边有个办公室。宏从那里经过了好几次，朝办公室里面看着。一个男人坐在窗边，在他上方有三四个电视屏幕，但是他对桌子上展开的报纸更感兴趣。

确定没有人看到后，宏赶快从办公室窗子底下过去，然后绕过了金属栏杆。非常简单，他进来了！

第78页

在停车场的一边他看到了一排名贵的汽车，在另一边一个牌子上写着“Ablieferungen”。宏不知道是什么意思，但是过了一会儿来了一辆白色的大厢式货车，车的一侧有水果和蔬菜的图片。宏猜自己一定在宾馆的厨房附近，他刚才看到的那个牌子是“送货”的意思。

就在他前面，有说话声。宏在一辆汽车后面蹲下来，仔细看着下一个拐角周围。两个小伙子站在门外边，抽着烟。他们穿着厨房工人的白色上衣，看起来有一点儿偷偷摸摸的，仿佛在违反什么规定。宏就等在那里，观察着。

五分钟后，他们有说有笑地进去了。宏又等了半分钟，然后跑到门口，就是刚才那两个小伙子消失的地方。门仍然半开着，他推门进去，发现自己在一个狭窄的走廊里。

他能听到前面厨房里的声音。他往前移动着。在走廊的中间处，左边有一个门。他停下来，听了听，没有声音，于是小心翼翼地打开门，往里面看去。

第79页

有一面墙上只有一个长搁架，上面放着一大罐一大罐的食品罐头，但是当他往房间的另一边看时，他简直不能相信自己有这般运气。在另一扇门后面，宏看到三四件白色上衣，与刚才抽烟的人穿的衣服很像。宏想，如果他穿上其中一件，或许能够毫无阻拦地穿过厨房。

没有时间继续想了。宏试了第一件上衣，太大了。他把它放回去，拿了下一件，这一件正好。他迅速把纽扣自下而上扣到领口，然后径直朝门口走去。

接着他停住了。如果他手里拿着什么东西或许会更好，这样他被拦住的可能性会更小。他转过身去，拿起两大罐食品罐头，接着他决定拿第三罐，因为这能遮住他一半儿的脸。然后他就从门口出去了。

他走得很快。他不能停下来四处张望，必须显得很清楚自己要去哪儿。他只能相信自己的运气。

令他惊讶的是，整个过程就像梦一样。宏沿着走廊一直走，几秒钟以后，他发现自己到了一个大厨房。右边有三个男人站在烤箱附近，但是他们甚至没有抬头看，每个人都在忙着自己的工作。

第80页

宏径直往前走，然后走到一扇半开着的门前。这时，他听到一个人正从另一个方向进来。宏立刻转过身来用背推开门走了出去——他正拿着东西，这样做是最自然不过的了。另一个男人匆忙经过，一句话都没有说。

从门口一出来，宏就发现自己到了一个大厅里，左边和右边都有更多的门，长长的走廊几乎望不到头，在他前面有楼梯和电梯门。

宏考虑乘电梯。如果这是只供宾馆工作人员使用的工作电梯，它可能会一直通到楼顶。他深吸了口气，按了按钮。电梯的门马上开了。他走进去，接着又出来了。他一直拿着的食品罐头刚才有用，但是现在他需要别的东西。

宏把食品罐头放在楼梯下面，然后注意到那儿有一堆脏床单。如果他拿着床单，宏希望他可以再次被误以为是宾馆的工作人员。他拿起床单，就在电梯门要关上时，进了电梯。他环顾四周找按钮。是的，正如他所猜测的！地下有两层，地上有七层。如果他的好运能继续就好了。当然，319 房间理应在第三层！

第81页

他按了显示“3”的按钮，电梯开始上行。

第 15 章　初识舒伯特

第82页

电梯停了，宏走了出来，发现自己在一个仅供员工使用的小区域。电梯对面是一扇门。宏推开门，下一刻，就像是通过了藏在墙里的秘密入口一样，他来到了宾馆的公共走廊。他在走廊中间的位置。走廊地面铺着深红色的地毯，向两侧延伸出去。

宏不知道往哪个方向走。他选了一个方向，但是看到门上的数字在变大：325、327、329。于是他转过身来，门上的数字开始变小，左边是偶数，右边是奇数。他顺着房间号走：325、323、321。当他走过最后这个房间，他感到自己的心脏开始狂跳。

突然间他到了，319 房间。正要敲门，他突然停了下来。当意识到自己不知要说什么、做什么的时候，他的自信一下子就不见了。他真的如此确定谋杀即将发生吗？

第83页

宏没有听到他身后的房门开了。忽然间他听到用德语说话的声音。

宏转身看到一个大约 30 岁的男人站在 320 房间门口。那个男人看起来很健壮，或许像个士兵，但是穿着便装。

宏感到无助。“对不起，我不懂德语。”他用英语说。

那个男人看起来很困惑。“你不会说德语？”

“不会。”宏说。

那个男人的眼睛眯了起来。“可是你在这儿工作？”

宏感到膝盖发软。他忘了自己穿着白上衣，拿着床单。现在他想不出该如何解释。“不，我是个学生，”他小声说，“但是我必须见到住在这个房间的人，就是施密特先生。我有重要的信息要告诉他。”

那个男人的身体马上紧绷起来。“我认为你最好先告诉我。我是施密特先生的同事。”

宏不知道该说什么。

“嗯，我在等你说。”那个男人继续说。

第84页

宏不确定自己是否可以信任这个男人，但是没有时间做决定了，宏不得不给出一个解释。“我来见施密特先生是因为……”他开始说，又停了，“嗯，他可能有生命危险。”

此时，这个男人的目光变得非常犀利。“咱们最好到我房间里去谈这件事情。”片刻后他说。他的声音明显是不容宏质疑的。

男人往后站了站，让宏进入他的房间。一进房间，男人就迅速关上门，然后从猫眼看了看外面的走廊。

“请坐。”那个男人转身对宏说。

宏把床单放在门后，选了把最近的椅子。

那个男人立刻继续说：“好，你说你是个学生？”他没有坐下来，也没有等宏回答。“那么，你要告诉施密特先生什么信息？”

“我在来柏林的火车上，”宏用颤抖的声音开始说，“偶然看了一个男人的手机，看到一条信息——实际上是两条信息，说的是今天晚上在这家宾馆的 319 房间的一个任务。”

第85页

那个男人看起来很惊讶。“继续。”他迅速说。

“嗯，火车上的那个男人，他试图杀死我。他现在就在宾馆里，就在二十分钟前我看到他了。”

听到这里，那个男人拉过另外一把椅子，坐得离宏很近。他的声音变得十分严肃。“这不是一个学生开的玩笑，对吧？”他说，“这很重要，你明白吗？”

“是的，我明白。”宏直视着男人的眼睛。“我还被绑架了，”过了一会儿他补充道，“我一直很害怕。”

那个男人停顿了一下，然后点点头。“你知道施密特先生的真实身份吗？”

宏摇摇头。“不知道。您是什么意思？难道施密特不是他的真名吗？”

“不，不是真名。”那个男人仔细地注视着宏。他考虑了一会儿，继续说：“听着，我要告诉你一些可能我不应该说的事情，但是好像没有时间了，所以我不得不冒这个险。施密特先生是谁不重要，只要知道他是一个极其重要的人物就够了。由于种种我不能解释的原因，施密特先生住在这家宾馆是保密的。”

“好的。”宏回答。

第86页

“嗯，我是他的保镖，他的私人保镖，我在这里确保他的安全。正常情况下，他会带多名保镖，但是因为他是秘密地来到这里，所以我是今天晚上他身边唯一的保镖，懂了吗？”

宏点点头。

那个男人现在非常严肃，他往前坐了坐，凑近宏。“那么，来杀他的这个男人是谁？他长什么样子？”

宏咳嗽了一下。有一秒钟时间他说不出话来。“他很老……但是他身上真的有种令人害怕的东西。他像鲨鱼——他长着鲨鱼一样的眼睛和牙齿。在火车上，他说他叫埃里克·比约恩森，自称是一个商人，但是他今天晚上打扮成牧师的样子进了宾馆。”

“牧师！”那个男人重复道。

“是的，我确定。”宏回答。

那个男人从椅子上一跃而起，走到门口。他从猫眼观察了一会儿，接着后退几步。他思考了一两秒钟，又说话了：“好，听着，没有时间去叫我同事了，所以我需要你的帮助。你的手机号是什么？”

宏此时觉得很害怕，但是他也有一种很棒的感觉，他不再是孤军奋战了——终于有人相信他了。他跟男人说了自己的手机号，男人把它输入了自己的手机里。他立刻按了“呼叫”键，宏的手机响了起来，接着又停了。

第87页

“好，”那个男人说，“现在你也有我的手机号了。”他停顿了一下，然后又坐到宏的对面。“好，我想让你这样做。我会试着让总——我是说，施密特先生，离开这个地方，或者至少换到别的房间。我想让你留在这里，站在门口通过猫眼观察外面。如果这个家伙——也就是这个牧师——出现，你一看到他，就给我打电话，明白了吗？”

“明白。”宏回答。

“好。”那个男人坐直身子，他看了宏一秒钟，又说：“你叫什么名字？”

“足立宏。”

“我叫舒伯特，弗朗兹·舒伯特。”那个男人说着立刻抬起手，

“是的，我知道，有一位著名的作曲家名字跟我一样。我父母对古典音乐很痴狂。不管怎样，请叫我弗朗兹。”

“好的，弗朗兹。”宏说。

“太好了。”舒伯特回应道。他把手搭在宏的肩膀上。“你做得很出色，宏。你非常勇敢。”

第88页

他不再耽误时间。他向宏点了点头，站起来，拿起墙边的一个小包，走到门口。“好的，就是这样。”他说。与此同时，他把手伸进夹克，掏出了一把枪。这种黑色金属给人一种非常冰冷的感觉。然后他把手臂垂到一侧。“十五分钟后见。”他低声说。

下一刻男人已经离开了。房间里一片寂静。

宏看着门。他突然充满了恐惧，他又是独自一人了。

第 16 章　牧师到访

第89页

宏站在那里盯着门看了五六秒钟，突然想起他有任务要做。他不再浪费时间，通过猫眼观察着。

视野比他预想的要好，除了对面的 319 房间，他还能看到走廊几米外的地方。舒伯特此刻就在那里。宏能看到他正前后观察着走廊，手枪仍垂在他身旁。

大约十秒钟以后，319 房间的门开了。一位身穿红色睡袍的非常迷人的金发女郎站在门口。她跟舒伯特交谈了一会儿，接着面带担忧地返回房间。舒伯特跟她一起进了房间，门立刻关上了。

一分钟过去了。宏除了确认手机上“最后通话”是舒伯特的号码外，就一直盯着门。

第90页

当他重新看向猫眼时，外面走廊上有个人进入了他的视野。宏的心脏跳得更快了。会是鲨鱼吗？宏更加仔细地观察着。不，是一个十六七岁的男孩儿，穿着一身整洁的宾馆制服。他手里端着一个金属盘子，上面放着一张便条，但是他会不会是鲨鱼的同伙儿？宏通过猫眼观察着，这个男孩儿直接来到宏的门口，敲了敲门。

宏不知道该怎么办。他不想开门，但是这人可能真的是宾馆工作人员，或许这张便条很重要，是舒伯特应该知道的。宏看到那个男孩儿朝走廊看了看，接着听到他又敲了敲门，敲得更使劲儿了。

这一次宏决定做出回应。他小心翼翼地开了门。门仅开到一半，就传来两声闷响："咚！咚！"一声接着一声。与此同时那个男孩儿好像把自己抛到了宏身上，他的双臂就像恋人一样扑过来环抱着他。宏被撞得往后一趔趄，撞到墙上，接着倒在了地板上。那个男孩儿压在他身上，一动不动地躺在那里。他端的盘子砰的一声撞在门上。

宏努力站起来。他蒙了，以至于有三四秒钟时间他还没意识到那个男孩儿遭到枪击了。接着另一个人出现在门口，是鲨鱼。他仍然打扮成牧师的样子，但是此时他提着一把消音枪。宏想说话，但是嘴里发不出任何声音来。

第91页

"是的，我的朋友，是我，"鲨鱼带着令人作呕的微笑说，"我为我的暴力入侵表示歉意。"他把那个年轻的宾馆服务员的腿踢到一边，然后立刻关上门。"最倒霉的年轻人。我需要用某种方式让你开门，"他继续说，"这个男孩儿很不幸，我选择了他。"然后，他蹲下来，与宏保持水平。他继续说："好，现在听着，我的日本朋友，我没有时间了。我看到你进了这个房间，现在我需要一些信息。"

宏还在努力平复呼吸，他从尸体下挣脱出来。这时，宏发现自己的牛仔裤上全是血。有一瞬间他以为自己在流血，随后他意识到血是那个宾馆服务员的。一声尖叫在宏的嗓子里膨胀，却喊不出来。

鲨鱼把脸凑向宏。他的牙齿看上去很亮。"很快我就会杀了你。"

第92页

宏完全说不出话来。

鲨鱼点点头。"是的，这是肯定的，我会杀了你，但是我可以用两种方式。"他凑得更近了。"第一种是把子弹打在脑袋中间，就像这样……"他把枪顶到宏的额头中间，舌头发出咔嗒的声音，然后把枪拿开。"你什么都感觉不到，非常干净利落——你会喜欢的！"他停顿了一下。"或者我可以打你的肚子。这种痛是很可怕的，请相信我。"想到这里，他的眼睛好像闪烁着快乐的光芒。"是的，非常可怕。这就是为什么你们日本人会把刀插进肚子'切腹自杀'——因为死得很慢，会受很多罪。非常勇敢，你们日本人。"

第93页

这时鲨鱼往后蹲坐在自己脚后跟上，若有所思地盯着宏。"那么这就由你选择了，我的朋友。如果你把我想知道的告诉我，'砰、砰'打在脑袋上，一切都很快。如果你不这样做，你会死得很慢。所以，你选择哪一种？"

鲨鱼说话的时候，宏一直在拼命想自己该怎么办，什么也做不了吗？结局真的是这样吗？这一整天他都在置自己于险境，但不知为什么似乎并不真实，几乎就像一个电脑游戏，玩够了就可以把它关掉。现在的情形是完全真实的。他想要抱怨之前没有解释清楚游戏规则，但是他知道这无济于事。他突然想到了秋子，他终究是再也见不到她了吗？

第94页

“所以，你选哪一种？”鲨鱼使劲儿把枪顶到宏的肚子上，笑了。

宏没有回答。想到秋子，他突然有了主意。他的手机还握在手里。他能做到不看按键就给舒伯特打电话吗？他对自己的手机了如指掌，包括所有按键的位置和功能。如果他能把手伸进口袋，就能避开鲨鱼的视线。他需要做的就是按出舒伯特的号码，按下“呼叫”键。

鲨鱼在等他的答案。“嗯？”

“你想知道什么？”宏迅速说。

鲨鱼看起来很惊讶。“所以，你选择脑袋！这很好。对，我需要知道这个。”

宏设法靠着墙坐起来，他已经把手放进口袋里握住手机了。他将手机在手里转过来。手机的方向握得对吗？他不得不摸索着按键，但是不能按得太用力。

“那个进入319房间的男人，”鲨鱼开始问，“他是个保镖，是吗？”

“是的。”宏回答。手机的方向是对的，他很确定。好的，现在要按出舒伯特的号码，他必须按“返回”键。

第95页

“他是唯一的保镖，是吗？”

“是的。”宏回答。他的手指在按键区摸索着，在右上角，这就是要按的键。他毫不迟疑地按了下去。

“保镖为什么进了那个房间？”

宏停顿了一下。“他要把施密特先生转移到另一个房间，我觉得。”

鲨鱼发出了一声短促的笑声。“施密特！哈！那很好。那个保镖找帮手了吗？”

宏没回答。他正在努力考虑手机的问题。“呼叫”键——在左上角，不是吗？是吧？突然他没那么确定了。

“快说！”鲨鱼的眼睛里突然充满了愤怒。“回答我！会有更多的人来吗？他们知道我的长相吗？”

“不知道！”宏回答，“我不知道，我认为他们不知道。”

“你在撒谎！你告诉他我打扮成了牧师，是吗？”

宏正要回答，这时他记起来了，“呼叫”键不在最上面，而是它下面那个。

“嗯？”鲨鱼喊道。

“有可能。”宏轻声说。

“啊，终于说实话了！”鲨鱼向后坐了一会儿，看起来很高兴。“无论如何，这无关紧要。我得到了我需要的信息。”他又往前坐了坐。“我的朋友，时间到了。我很遗憾不能再深入了解你了，你看起来是个很勇敢的小伙子，但是……”鲨鱼举起双手，仿佛是在道歉。

第96页

宏很害怕，他又一次感到喉咙发紧。他的手指又滑过手机的按键，这个对吗？他找到正确的按键了吗？没有时间再想了，他用大拇指使劲儿摁了下去。

鲨鱼举起枪指着宏的脑袋。

宏觉得自己可能会哭。他必须让鲨鱼一直说话。要过多久舒伯特才会接呢？舒伯特是宏最后的希望了。

“等一下！”宏绝望地喊，“求求你，求求你，我知道你要杀我，但是你能为我做一件事情吗？”

那个老头儿突然摆出一副慈祥模样。“临终遗愿？”他的眼睛又眯了起来。“是什么？”

宏必须让鲨鱼再多说几秒钟。他说出了浮现在脑海里的第一件事情。“是我的女朋友，秋子。来柏林之前我们刚分手。你能替我给她发一条信息吗？”

“哈！”鲨鱼突然笑了，“多浪漫啊！现在我要让一对恋人在地狱相会了。”

第97页

宏无法呼吸，或许他把按键全搞错了，或许没有任何希望了……

“你希望我发什么催人泪下的信息？”鲨鱼又做出关心的表情。

“请告诉她……”宏开始说。

“什么？”鲨鱼说。

“我想让你告诉她……”宏重新开始说。

鲨鱼突然厌烦了这个游戏。“呸！你想浪费时间。你以为我傻吗？”

“不！”宏喊着。突然微弱的声音传来，是从宏的口袋里发出来的。

房间里安静了一秒钟。

随后声音又出现了，是有人在说话。“宏？”声音很小，接着变大了。“宏，我是弗朗兹！”

第 17 章　不速之客

第98页

“那是什么声音？”鲨鱼厉声问道。

“我不知道。”宏撒谎说。他能听到舒伯特在反复叫他的名字。

“是你的手机！”鲨鱼说。他的眼睛里充满怒火。“把它给我！”

宏非常缓慢地从口袋里掏出手机。

舒伯特的声音一下子变得清楚了。“宏？宏？什么情况？”宏几乎不敢相信，计划成功了！

但是鲨鱼此时正怒火中烧。他用外语喊了一个宏听不懂的词，接着又用英语说：“你做了什么？你给这个人打电话了！”他的枪就在宏的眼前晃着。鲨鱼的脸色突然变得非常冷峻。

完了，宏想。开枪的时候到了。现在舒伯特已不再说话，或许此刻他正穿过走廊，或许他会随时破门而入，但是那个保镖现在做什么都没用了。宏知道太晚了。他无助地抬起一只手挡在脸前，仿佛在幻想能挡住子弹。他准备好遭受枪击了。

第99页

但是鲨鱼并没有开枪。相反，他把手机从宏的手里夺过来。

“你是谁？”鲨鱼愤怒地对着手机说。

宏听不到舒伯特回答的是什么。枪还在指着宏的脑袋，宏很难进行思考。

“好，”鲨鱼换了语气轻声说道，“听我说，我相信你知道你在跟谁说话，你肯定知道，这个日本男孩儿在我手上。如果你试图做任何蠢事，我就立刻毙了他，清楚了吗？”

宏推测舒伯特回答他了，但是他不知道舒伯特说了什么。鲨鱼打断了他。

“好了，闭嘴！听我说，我要带着这个男孩儿离开宾馆，你不能做任何阻拦，我已经杀了一个宾馆服务员了。现在，这是我想要的。你在仔细听吗？”他迅速站起来，朝门口走去，通过猫眼看了看外面。接着他走到窗口，朝外面的夜色看去。他一直用枪指着宏，很快就走了回来。

第100页

“几分钟后，我和这个男孩儿要离开这个房间。我们要下楼去宾馆后面的入口——你叫一辆出租车在那里等着我们，我会告诉司机去哪儿，但是你不要试图跟踪出租车。如果在任何一点上出差错，这个日本男孩儿就会死，清楚吗？我给你三分钟时间去安排。一切准备就绪之后，给我回电话。”

鲨鱼按了“结束通话”键，把手机放进了自己的口袋，然后他望着宏。“这并不意味着你最终能活下来，”他说，“如果可以，我会杀你两次！”

听着鲨鱼的话，宏感觉自己已经莫名其妙地死去了。他太累了，过去的二十四小时过得如此艰难，好像在观看一部疯狂的电影，无能为力地看着电影演绎自己的人生故事。

“站起来！”鲨鱼一边说，一边又拿着枪朝他走来。

宏慢慢地爬起来。他想知道接下来会发生什么。

“现在，到门那边去，把那个男孩儿挪开。”鲨鱼命令道。

第101页

宏又感觉不舒服。他挪过去，伸手去拉那个男孩儿的胳膊。直到那时他才意识到那个男孩儿真的死了。除了自己的爷爷，这是宏第一次看到死人。当他努力抬起男孩儿的肩膀时，他感觉他的肩膀很沉，很暖。真的没有生命了吗？就在十分钟以前，这个男孩儿还在高兴地敲他的门。宏想哭。

鲨鱼死死地盯着他。"第一次？"他冷冷地问，"不要害怕，死人往往不会抱怨。"他露出牙齿笑了一会儿，样子非常恐怖。然后他的脸又变得冷峻起来。"快点儿，不要浪费时间。"

宏用胳膊揽着尸体用力拉。"对不起。"他小声说。最终尸体移开了。宏在地毯上拖着男孩儿，后面留下一条长长的鲜红色血迹。宏觉得自己快要吐了。

片刻后，宏的手机在鲨鱼的口袋里又响了起来。宏看到鲨鱼把手伸进衣服里，接着突然发生了一连串的事情。首先是一道强光和一次恐怖的爆炸，接着房间彻底黑了。与此同时，一团烟雾充满了房间。宏听到了枪声，又是消音枪的"砰！砰！"声，然后是"啊！"的一声大叫，紧接着是家具撞碎的声音。之后是一片出奇的安静，就像世界末日一样。有那么一会儿，宏在想自己是否已经死了。

第102页

这时灯又亮了。

过了一会儿，房间里的烟雾才散掉。这时，宏看到房间的门没有了。门落在地板上，成了碎片。舒伯特站在门上面。他对面的地板上躺着鲨鱼。那个老头儿还活着，但是他正紧紧地捂着腹部，鲜血已经开始从他那身牧师的衣服上渗出来，无论他使多大劲儿捂着，似乎都不能止住血。

"抱歉我没有敲门就进来了。"舒伯特冷冷地说。

鲨鱼的眼睛痛苦地紧闭着。他缓慢地扭过头，直视着宏。他面色苍白如纸，但是他的牙齿在明亮的灯光下仍然闪着光。

他用微弱的声音说：“我真希望在火车上选了别的座位。”

第 18 章　致谢便条

第103页

第二天下午两点钟，宏和舒伯特坐在广播塔餐厅。这家餐厅位于柏林施潘道区著名的广播电视塔的半中腰。这是晴好的一天，阳光灿烂，从那上面可以远眺这座城市——车辆如梭的宽阔马路、公园，甚至远在城市之外的湖泊和森林都能看到。远处有一架喷气式飞机刚刚从机场爬升到空中，好像钉在了天上，一动不动。

“这家餐厅以海鲜出名，”舒伯特看着菜单说，“为什么我们不点那个？”

“太贵了。”宏回答，他注意到了价格。

“不要担心价格，”舒伯特迅速说，“有个大款会买单，咱们尽情享用吧！”

讨论结束后，舒伯特跟服务员点了菜。服务员离开后，舒伯特看向窗户。“瞧，柏林也没有那么差，是不是？”他指着眼前的景色说。

第104页

宏正要回答，这时舒伯特的手机响了。他安静地听了大约半分钟，接着表示歉意后离开去了餐厅一个安静的区域，以便继续谈话。

舒伯特不在的时候，宏回想着当天早晨发生的事情。他们大部分时间都待在舒伯特的总部。“德国联邦宪法保卫局——国土安全部门。”舒伯特解释道。在那里，宏花了两个小时在电脑屏幕前看记录在案的罪犯的照片。宏唯一能确定指认的是那个跟迈耶一起接他上车的司机。宏很失望，但是舒伯特并不这么觉得，一旦他们找到了这个人，他神秘地说，抓住迈耶和其他人就容易了。

随后舒伯特说到午餐时间了。舒伯特将一个蓝色的警灯放在他的宝马车顶部，他们快速驶过柏林的街道，像一对傻小子那样笑着。这段旅途让宏感觉比之前的几周都要开心，而且很重要。

现在，坐在餐厅里，手里拿着饮料，宏发现很难相信发生的这一切。他向外眺望着这座城市，此刻觉得如此安全和放松。鲨鱼真的试图杀他吗？就像一场梦一样。这一切真的发生了吗？

第105页

仿佛是回应宏的思绪，舒伯特回到桌边坐下来。他看了看宏才开口。

“他死了。”他说。

宏困惑了片刻。

“我们的朋友，鲨鱼，他一个小时前死了。”

“哦。”宏说。那种感觉就像一只冰冷的手从他的背上滑落。“很遗憾。”他说。

“不要遗憾，”舒伯特很快回答说，“那个人是个职业杀手。他靠杀人谋生，他也差点儿把你杀了。”

“是的，我知道。”宏回答。

“无论如何，咱们叫他的真名吧。刚刚有人告诉我他其实是个挪威人，叫卡尔-亨里克·约翰森。国际刑警组织，就是国际警察，显然已经找他好几年了。他因十一起谋杀案被通缉，其中一个目标是南美某个国家的总统。”

宏不知道说什么。他不断回想起最后一次见到鲨鱼的样子，当时老头儿正被抬到救护车上，他疼得脸色惨白。

第106页

“当然，因为他来自国外，所以他需要在勃兰登堡门从迈耶那儿取枪，带枪入境太危险了。”

宏沉默了。现在每次提到枪，宏就想起那个年轻的宾馆服务员。

舒伯特关切地看着宏。“怎么了？”他低声问，“是那个男孩儿吗？”

宏点点头。“我不断想起……”

舒伯特伸出手臂。“试着不要去想那件事了，”他很温和地补充说，“如果这能有一点儿帮助，我可以告诉你，他没有受罪——他是瞬间被杀死的——子弹穿过了他的心脏。”

两个人都沉默了一会儿。

宏努力去想别的事情。当又觉得平静了一些时，他说：“我很惊讶，发生了这些事情后，鲨鱼还是决定继续刺杀计划。”

“是的，这是一个糟糕的错误。”舒伯特看着宏。“我想他不喜欢输给一个孩子……”一瞬间，舒伯特好像很尴尬，然后很快继续说道：“对不起，我不是说你是个孩子，但是我猜鲨鱼是那样看你的。你很聪明，你知道的，”舒伯特补充说，“你的行为非常非常特别。”

第107页

现在轮到宏尴尬了。幸运的是，这时服务员来了，所以宏不需要回应。一大盘海鲜摆在他的面前，宏突然意识到自己饿极了。

“Guten Appetit（德语，‘祝你好胃口’）。”舒伯特说。

“Itadakimasu（日语，‘我开动了’）。”宏回答。

他们都没说话，开心地吃了一会儿。然后舒伯特靠后坐着，仔细地看着宏。

“宏，我需要跟你谈一下施密特先生，”他开始说，“你是如此神勇，你应当知道一些关于他的事情，这样才公平。但是我很抱歉，我仍然不能告诉你他的真名，不过我要说，你救的这个人非常非常重要。”

“他在政府工作吗？”宏问。

舒伯特直视着宏。“我不能说，但他是顶级重要的人物。”

“你也不能告诉我为什么鲨鱼被雇来杀他吧，我猜……”宏说。

舒伯特无可奈何地笑了笑。“重要的人物就有重要的敌人。我们认为迈耶的人数月来一直在企图刺杀施密特。先前的计划失败后，他们似乎决定要雇最厉害的杀手——那就是，鲨鱼。”

第108页

宏困惑了。“那为什么……为什么施密特在宾馆只带着你一个人？为什么他要秘密地去那儿？”

舒伯特看上去又尴尬了。过了一会儿，他往前坐了坐。“有时候，宏，一个像施密特先生这样的人希望自己的生活有一部分私密空间，所以他才会在宾馆里见朋友，所以我是宾馆里唯一的保镖。你能理解我说的吗？”

宏突然想起那位打开施密特的宾馆房门的金发女郎。“你的意思是……”他慢慢地说。

“不知迈耶和他的同伙儿怎么发现了施密特先生的……”舒伯特搜索着恰当的词语说道，“施密特先生的安排。他们发现后，看到了一个杀他的机会。”

宏盯着舒伯特，这个男人告诉了他尽可能多的信息。宏点点头。“我想我懂了，谢谢你告诉我。”

舒伯特摇摇头。“不，不，我们必须谢谢你。”他稍微咳嗽了一下。“事实上，说到了那个话题，我有些东西要给你。”他把手伸进口袋，掏出一个信封，在手里拿了一会儿。

第109页

“施密特先生让我把这个给你。”舒伯特说着把信封递了过去。

宏看了它一会儿。

“来，打开它。”舒伯特说。

宏照他说的做了。里面还有一个信封和一张手写的小便条，便条用英语写着：

“非常感谢你为我做的一切。你是一位真正的‘武士’。旅途愉快。”

便条的署名只有一个词：“施密特”。

宏放下便条，打开了第二个信封，里面有十张崭新的五百欧元纸币。

第 19 章　友好的建议

第111页

两个小时后，享用完美味的午餐，宏和舒伯特乘电梯回到地面。他们钻进舒伯特的宝马车里，启程回市中心去。舒伯特一点儿都不着急，这一次他开得慢很多，并摇下车窗，享受着阳光。

在午餐和施密特给的钱带来的兴奋感消失之后，宏突然感觉到莫名的空虚。他有一种奇怪的感觉，感觉自己终于要回到现实生活了。从某种意义上来说这很好，知道自己平安无事真的很棒，但是回到现实还意味着记起他与秋子的分手。他多希望能与她分享施密特的礼物啊！

好像舒伯特能够看透他的心思。紧接着，舒伯特一边开车一边看向他问道："那么，我的朋友，你决定怎么花这笔钱了吗？"

宏咬了咬嘴唇。他扭过头向窗外看去。"我不确定，"他低声说，"我想我可能把它存起来。"

第112页

"什么？"舒伯特喊道，"拜托！不要这么无聊，至少要享受一部分。飞去什么地方吧！去个特别的地方！带着你女朋友！"

舒伯特的话再糟糕不过了。一时间宏以为自己可能会哭出来——过去的二十四小时已经消耗了他所有的力气。这次他用力咬了一下嘴唇，以至于尝到了血的味道。

舒伯特注意到了。"嘿，我说错话了吗？"他更加温和地问。

宏觉得太累了，他无力撒谎。"我跟女朋友分手了，就在我来这儿之前。"他最后说。

舒伯特看起来很尴尬。"对不起，"他小声补充说，"那是她提的，不是你吧？"

宏点点头。"我仍然不知道这是怎么发生的。我觉得我们在一起真的很开心。"当所有的回忆涌上心头，他闭上了眼睛。

沿着这条路开了一百米，舒伯特把车停了下来。"你为什么不跟我说说呢？"他说，"发生了什么？"

宏睁开眼睛。他们来到一个公园旁边，他能看到远处一对年轻情侣手牵着手穿过树林。

"我就是不明白。"宏开始说。他又摇了摇头。"我们发生了一次可怕的争执。我们本计划一起度假，接着，不知怎么回事，这场糟糕的战争开始了。"

第113页

“继续。”舒伯特说。

“嗯，这听起来很荒唐，但是这与我的狗有关。我有一条狗，名字叫小雪，是一条金毛猎犬。总之，我把它的照片放到手机里当屏保了。我女朋友认为应该换成她的照片。我不能理解她怎么能吃一条狗的醋。”

舒伯特脸上露出古怪的表情。“真的吗？这听起来不像是一个分手的好理由，你确定没有其他事情了？”

宏回过头看着舒伯特。“你是什么意思？”

“嗯，人们并不总是有话直说，宏。拜托，你知道的，女孩子最不想有话直说！大概还有其他原因。”

宏努力回想。他能丝毫不差地回忆起整个争执的过程。他到她房间里跟她说话，告诉她自己邀请了大次郎和阿玉木及他们的女朋友一起旅行。秋子对此没什么意见，她说：“棒极了，真好。”她还说：“人越多越好！”她不像是介意……她不……

舒伯特打断了宏的思绪。“想到了什么？”

“我刚刚想到一些事情。在我们做旅行计划时，我想如果我们邀请一些其他人会很棒。你不认为……？”

第114页

“继续。”舒伯特说。

“嗯，是两个男孩儿和他们的女朋友。你不会以为她为这个吃醋吧，会吗？”宏问。就在他说这些话时，一个可怕的想法闪过脑海。阿玉木的女朋友是莉萨。莉萨跟宏来自日本同一所大学，他曾经约她出去过。可能秋子发现这件事儿了，或许她以为……

舒伯特看着宏摇了摇头。“天哪，我的朋友，”他说，“在国际刺杀案上，你可能太聪明了，但是似乎一个年轻姑娘就让你招架不住了。你们在计划一个浪漫的二人假期，然后你又邀请了另外两个姑娘同行。我猜这两个女孩儿很漂亮吧？”

宏突然感到非常不舒服。“还好。”他回答，稍微咳嗽了一下。

“嗯，当然，她吃醋了！”舒伯特插话说，“她只是假装是那条狗的原因，所以她就不用承认是因为女孩儿们了，后来呢？”

“她说她永远不想再见到我了。”宏回答。

“所以，你相信她了，我猜。作为一个勇敢的‘武士’，你自尊心太强，不愿再给她打电话。我猜你没有道歉吧？”舒伯特问。

第115页

宏什么也没说。他对舒伯特感到又爱又恨。这个男人让他觉得自己极度愚蠢和渺小。

舒伯特看着宏，大约十秒钟两人都没说一句话。然后舒伯特又说：“好吧，我的朋友，你为我做了一些事情，现在我要为你做点儿事情。拿出你的手机。”

宏没有争辩。

“现在给我找出她的号码。”舒伯特命令道。

宏的心脏剧烈跳动起来。他选了“菜单”键，又找到“电话本”，然后找到了秋子的号码。

“好。”舒伯特下了车。他绕到副驾，打开车门，然后坚定地说：“好，下来吧。”宏按照他说的做了。

舒伯特指向对面的公园。“你看到那边的座位了吗？你走过去坐在那里，然后拨打那个号码。”

宏意识到他的嘴唇在颤抖。“我要说什么啊？”

“你会想出来的。”舒伯特回答。

有一会儿工夫，宏没有动，然后他感觉到舒伯特的手放在他的背上，把他推过去了。

第116页

宏沿着小路慢慢走着。他的腿感觉很沉重，几乎沉得走不动了。太阳也火辣辣地烤着他的脖颈儿，他感觉吃的那些食物让他有点儿恶心。最后他来到座位跟前，坐了下来。

他看着对面的汽车。舒伯特又坐回车里去了，正透过窗户看着。宏几乎紧张得像鲨鱼拿枪指着他的头一样。他看着手机和秋子的照片，然后深吸了口气。

几秒钟以后，他按下了“呼叫”键。

